Last Days of the Bus Club

The fourth book in the
Driving Over Lemons trilogy

Chris Stewart

W F HOWES LTD

This large print edition published in 2014 by
W F Howes Ltd
Unit 4, Rearsby Business Park, Gaddesby Lane,
Rearsby, Leicester LE7 4YH

1 3 5 7 9 10 8 6 4 2

First published in the United Kingdom in 2014
by Sort Of Books

All photos © Sort Of Books on behalf of the photogtraphers:
Maggie Harris, Arezoo Farazad, Ana Exton, Carole Stewart,
Stefan Tolde, Martin Orbach, Pedro L. Barberá Briones, Andrew
Phillips and Mark Ellingham. Thanks to them all, and thanks
especially to Maggie for the photo shoots, to Nikky Twyman for
proofreading, Henry Iles for text design, Peter Dyer for cover
design, and Chris Andrews for the cover illustration.

A CIP catalogue record for this book is available
from the British Library

ISBN 978 1 47127 162 5

Typeset by Palimpsest Book Production Limited,
Falkirk, Stirlingshire

Printed and bound in Great Britain
by TJ International Ltd, Padstow, Cornwall

MIX
Paper from
responsible sources
FSC
www.fsc.org   FSC® C013056

For Michael Jacobs

my favourite travelling companion

CONTENTS

CHAPTER 1

LAST DAYS OF THE BUS CLUB

Through all the years of my daughter Chloé's schooling it fell to me to get the family ship under way in the morning. I function better in the early hours; Ana, my wife, lasts longer into the night than I do. And so it was that on a cool September morning, the first day of Chloé's last year at school, I rose in the dark. At six forty-five it's still dark where we live, in the mountains of Granada, as, even at summer's end, the sun takes its time rising above the cliffs behind our home. Leaving my wife and the dogs fast asleep in the bedroom, I padded across the cold stone floor to the bathroom, splashed my eyes with cold water, dressed, and went into the kitchen. I put the kettle on, lit the candles for the breakfast table and at seven o'clock I woke Chloé. In all the fourteen years of the school run I did not have to wake her again more than on one or two occasions. She loved school, and would appear without fail ten minutes later blinking in the candlelight and clutching her heavily stacked backpack.

Chloé's breakfast, a glass of freshly squeezed orange juice and a bowl of some absurd industrially modified cereal product – Choco Kreks, ideally – was already on the table, while I busied myself with the first task of the day: the preparation of her mid-morning sandwich. In the creation of these little masterpieces I employed all the imagination and artistry I possess. I couldn't bring myself to inflict upon my daughter the standard Spanish *bocadillo* – a dry and artless roll, unaccountably afforded the status of cultural icon in spite of its curious quality of emerging from the oven almost completely stale. No, for Chloé's delectation I would first select a better class of bun – and these are to be had, if you know where to look. (Supermercado Mercadona, top left corner of the bakery section, labelled 'Mini Ciabattas'.)

These I would slit open with a razor-sharp knife, leaving an infinitesimal hinge of crust. Then I would oil them up a bit with a little extra-double-virgin, cold-pressed, unfiltered, single-variety, single-estate olive oil from our own Picual trees, add a layer of thinly sliced tomatoes (ready salted to enhance the flavour), a dab of sugar to counteract the acidity, a couple of transparently thin slivers of fresh garlic, some Genoese basil, and finally a dollop of mayonnaise to help the whole concoction slip down . . . oh, and a few chives sticking out of the end like whiskers on a prawn.

This was the vegetarian option. There was a meat one, too, with exquisite *embutidos* – the preserved meats that the Spanish do rather well – enlivened by a scattering of sliced gherkins, some chilli sauce perhaps, and a handful of herbs. Or the oriental *bocadillo* with ginger, chutney, a prawn or two and some beansprouts.

I would then slip a couple of these into one of those silver bags that vacuum-packed coffee comes in; they fit perfectly and it made them smell of fresh coffee, which Chloé, especially when little, didn't like, but I thought would set her up for the future.

In truth these snacks were not always greatly to Chloé's taste. When young, she disliked being marked out as different from her peers, and would mournfully report that she had shared her *bocadillos* with her friends, and the friends, who were no doubt busy trying to get their teeth through their own stale dry buns, had not thought much of them. But gradually things changed, and Chloé, charged with the nostalgia teenagers develop for their infancy, increasingly accepted my creations for what they were – simple manifestations of love.

That morning, with an atmosphere of newness that comes with the first day back at school, the *bocadillos* crammed in amongst the books in Chloé's backpack, and the backpack on my back, we left the house to walk down the hill and across the valley, with Bumble and Bao, the dogs, sniffing the fresh morning scents behind us.

The first rays of sunshine were already warming the far side of the valley, as we walked past the stable, pausing to catch the cacophony of farting and coughing with which the sheep habitually start the day, and hastened upriver amongst the oleanders and tamarisk to the bridge. Our bridge, being a ramshackle contrivance of worm-eaten eucalyptus beams thrown across the river, has no railings, and tends to sag and creak if you creep gingerly across it. So we don't; casting caution to the side we leap down the bank and race across as fast as we can go. For late summer there was a good flow of red-tinged, iron-rich water rushing down the river. With only minutes to go now we scrambled into the aged Land Rover – no doors – and accelerated off along the sandy tracks in the riverbed, and up the hill towards the final stop on the school bus route, just above La Cenicera, the farm where our Dutch neighbour Bernardo lives.

Jesús, who keeps a flock of goats and sheep high up on Carrasco, the hill farm opposite us, was already there in his little white van, and Bernardo was leaning on its roof, chatting to him through the open window.

In a cloud of dust we hurtled past the little gathering and raced to get the car turned round before the bus came. The dust had hardly settled before the bus nosed cautiously round the corner. There was a rush and tumble of frantic kissing as Bernardo kissed his son Sebastian, Jesús kissed his boys José and Javier, and I kissed Chloé, and they climbed onto the bus, leaving us three fathers waving until it disappeared round the corner.

★   ★   ★

4

And so began the morning's meeting of the three fathers of the valley – Bernardo, Jesús and me – or the Bus Club, as I liked to call it. I think we all rather cherished being able once again to have these few minutes together at the start of a weekday; we had missed it over the long summer months. It gave us a chance to discuss what was going on in the valley, exchange what scant news there was from the town, and reminisce a little.

Inspired perhaps by the presence of a horrible-looking cur of a dog that was sniffing the wheel of Jesús's van, perhaps with a view to urinating in a small way against it, Bernardo was telling a scurrilous tale that featured dogs. We learned that he had a bitch on heat, and he had locked her in the bathroom in order to protect her from the lascivious attentions of the hordes of male curs who had travelled from the four corners of the province of Granada to press their suits.

'I locked 'er in de barfroom,' he said, 'because it's de only place wid a lock on de deur, an' dere wass orl dese doggs howlin' an' barkin' an' slobberin' about der place orl nite long an' I don't want 'em to get at 'er.'

'Very sensible,' Jesús and I concurred.

'Only when I come out in de mornin' de whole lot of 'em was down in de barfroom wid der bitch, dey gone an' dug a 'ole through de roof.'

'Ah,' I observed sagely. 'You can't lock the door on love, Bernardo.' Jesús grinned in agreement.

'Dat's not lurv,' exclaimed Bernardo, looking at us in amazement, 'Dat's jus' doggs fockin'.'

Of course we spoke in Spanish, because Jesús was limited to his native tongue, but I have written this little exchange in a sort of cod Dutch-English, in an attempt to give the flavour of Bernardo's Spanish, which is extremely good, but at least as idiosyncratic as my own.

Turning to Jesús, I asked after Ana and María-José, his two daughters. Not so long ago they too had waited for this same bus, like two baby birds they seemed, with backpacks on. But a couple of years ago they'd left to go to university in Granada. It's always a pleasure to ask Jesús about his daughters just to see the honest pride it stirs in him. When they were schoolgirls, Jesús would answer with a fond, if slightly mystified, expression, 'Oh, they're doing fine.' He wasn't even really sure what they were studying; it was so far removed from the experience of this hard-working man who had lived and raised his family by the strength of his arm and the milk of his goats. But the day that Ana and Maria-José took their seats in the lecture halls of Granada University – one to study Business Administration, the other Economics – was a giant step for their family and the valley, and it was felt by all of us. A generation earlier it would have been almost impossible for country girls like these to attend university; they would have been needed to help on the farm, and a farm's meagre returns would certainly not

6

have stretched to tuition fees and accommodation in the city.

'Ay, Cristóbal,' he said. 'Enjoy this year with Chloé while you can; it'll be gone in a flash and she'll be off.'

Bernardo nodded knowingly; his two eldest were also living in Granada, while Rosa his younger daughter, who used to be Chloé's playmate, was about to leave to work for an NGO in Colombia. It seemed that the children of the valley were disappearing fast. Though Jesús still had the two boys, and Bernardo his Sebastian, my days in the Bus Club were numbered. I changed the subject a little abruptly.

'I've got a lamb for you, Jesús, if you want it,' I said.

'Seems an odd time to be lambing.'

'I know, but we have a few out-of-season lambers, covered by a rogue ram. Anyway, one of them has twins and I don't think she's got enough milk for both of them. Have you got goats milking at the moment?'

'There's always goats to milk,' said Jesús with resignation. 'I'll be happy to take it.'

'Then I'll bring it to Bus Club tomorrow.'

And so saying, we all set off home to our respective breakfasts.

It was not many weeks after the beginning of the term that I got a call from Chloé's school. It was from the assistant head, no less, and she wondered if, as a local author accustomed to regaling the public on the subject of my books, I might like to give a talk to the Instituto classes?

'Of course,' I said. 'What do you want me to talk about?'

'Oh, whatever takes your fancy, really. We'll leave the subject up to you.'

Well, addressing the school would be *pan comido*, I thought (the Spanish say 'bread eaten' rather than 'a piece of cake'). You don't have to prepare a thing like this; you just turn up and do it.

Or perhaps not. For, when I told Chloé, she expressed some concern.

'You've got to prepare this speech, Dad,' she insisted. 'The Instituto class is only a year below me. They're my friends, or at any rate the younger brothers and sisters of my friends.'

This gave me pause for thought, for apart from not wishing to shame my daughter I was a great admirer of Órgiva's school and its staff. It had done what Ana and I considered an excellent job, despite the fact that when we enrolled Chloé, Spain had one of the worst education records in Western Europe, and Andalucía the worst in Spain. But due to some fortunate glitch round about the turn of the new century – a good headmaster and some inspirational teachers – San José de Calasanz was different.

Chloé was emerging from school with an easy sociability, a confidence in her own judgement and a laudable streak of anti-materialism bordering on

8

contempt for fashion brands and accessories. These qualities might have had something to do with our own attitudes, but the ideas were consolidated by her *pandilla* at school. And the *pandilla*, the gang of girls and boys with whom she hung out, taught her to deal easily and naturally with her fellow beings, and to be comfortable in her own skin in a peculiarly Mediterranean way. This counts for a lot, and I was proud of Chloé and deeply grateful to all those who had helped to bring her up.

Of course it had a lot to do with growing up as a Spaniard. A century or so ago, George Borrow, in his book *The Bible in Spain*, made the rather pertinent observation of the Spanish: 'that in their social intercourse no people in the world exhibit a juster feeling of what is due to the dignity of human nature, or better understand the behaviour which it behoves a man to adopt towards his fellow human beings. It is one of the few countries in Europe where poverty is not treated with contempt, and, I may add, where the wealthy are not blindly idolised.'

Well, that's what our daughter got from the village school. And she had a point about the speech: this was an important gig and I had to get it right. So I thought about it for a bit and hit on the theme of laughter and school.

You laugh all your days – and it's one of the very best things in life – but you don't often laugh the way you laughed when you were at school, that gut-busting, aching, joyous agony of laughter. The sort of laughter you have to contain at any cost, for fear that the humourless tyrant doing his level best to illuminate your darkness on subjects in which you had not the remotest interest – the use of the gerund, or the genetic codes of peas – might catch you at it and suggest that you might want to share the joke with the class. And to share the joke with the class was what you didn't want because you knew full well that the joke was crass as crass can be and you were only so horribly convulsed with laughter because you weren't supposed to be. That was laughter, and it left you sweating and limp like a used rag. It was so good that I devoted a considerable part of my school career to the pursuit of it. With hindsight it occurs to me that my lamentable academic performance might have had something to do with this.

Be that as it may, I thought I could advise my eager young audience to do the same, to make the most of that unrepeatable laughter. I would go on from there to recommend some more profitable activity, like reading, in order to give the impression that there was more to me than mere mindless frivolity.

In town a couple of days before the talk, I put this idea to one of the teachers, Dori, the mother of Chloé's best friend María. It didn't go down too well. She said that although she remembered that laughter from her youth, it was no longer the same; school was a much more serious business today. The world is different now, and its school-children would not be able to make much of what

I was blathering on about. Best perhaps to drop this theme.

So I dropped it, and wondered what to say instead. Nothing obvious presented itself and I wondered a little more, and then, as so often happens, I threw in my lot with an eleventh-hour inspiration. I had been mulling over the way in which Chloé and her friends, both boys and girls, seemed to treat one another as if they belonged to the same species. Having been to a single-sex boarding school in England, I had for many years harboured a certain envy for boys who went to school with girls, and consequently knew how to deal with them on a more or less equal footing. I decided there and then to address the school on the great benefits of co-education.

Now, my method with talks, whatever the language, is to sketch in some basic themes and leave the actual wording of the thing to fend for itself. That way, I imagine, I can achieve an element of spontaneity, and may even, seeing as I don't actually know what I'm about to say next, share a bit of interest in the matter with the audience.

So, as I drove along the narrow road to town, I cast my mind back to the momentous day when, after years at that boys' boarding school, I entered Crawley New Town's finest co-educational sixth-form college, and a giddy infatuated trance that was to last the best of two years. These were pleasing thoughts to mull upon, but before I knew it I was being led up the steps of the assembly

11

hall and confronted with a great rabble of youth milling about in the passages and aisles. Chloé was in the senior building, safely (as far as she was concerned) out of the way, but I could pick out a few friendly faces from the younger siblings of her friends and the families we knew in town.

There was a not altogether fruitful call to silence as the last few miscreants scrambled noisily to their seats. The teacher – it was Dori – introduced me and I was left alone. I looked out for a moment across the heaving sea of girls and boys, waiting for the muse. And then I was away like a clockwork monkey, relishing the Spanish idioms that sprang to my aid and using my foreignness to advantage. I managed to raise the odd snigger and giggle, but if the truth be told it was like getting blood out of a stone (to be fair, not much of what a fifty-something-year-old has to say is funny to a teenager). I talked about the advantages of small town life; I told a little moral tale; I recommended the road less travelled, and extolled, briefly – and cautiously – some of the virtues of the wild side; and then I launched into my great paean to co-educationalism.

I wasn't far into it when a minor linguistic problem presented itself: I was suddenly seized by a doubt that such a word actually existed in Spanish. Why should it? Just about all education was co-educational, so why should there be a special word for it? This thought brought me almost to a standstill. But I soldiered on.

My preferred strategy for this sort of situation

is to slide neatly into the circumlocution. Forget the grammar and the vocabulary, and, if things are getting really out of hand, even the meaning; I just launch myself confidently onto a tangential track. The muse carried me along as I talked in ever more discursive mode about the pleasures of the sexes mingling, the masculine conjoining with the feminine, both coming together to create a well-rounded person.

I'm not sure that even I had much of a sense of what this blather was adding up to, and the slightly bemused expression of my audience did little to reassure me. But I plunged heedlessly on with my peroration, ending with my certainty that it was going to school with both girls and boys that had rescued me at the last minute from the warped confines of my earlier single-sex schooling and that I was sure it would be the making of all of them, too.

'And that', I said, by way of winding up, 'is it.'

There was that dread pause while my local reputation as a speaker hung in the balance, and then, to my relief, a spattering of polite applause laced with a puzzling undertone of sniggering from the older kids, and Dori came up on stage, gave me a kiss and bundled me off.

'Phew,' I said, 'tough gig.' Or rather, I thought I said 'tough gig'. Dori was looking at me uncertainly. '*Un bolo duro*' is what I said, and that, as I subsequently discovered, does not mean 'tough gig' at all, but rather 'a hard skittle'.

*   *   *

13

However, a hard skittle turned out to be about right, when on the following day reports of my speech reached my daughter. She climbed off the bus with an uncharacteristically sour, if not hurt, expression on her face.

'Dad, don't you think there are some things that you and Mum might want to discuss with me first before going off and announcing them to the whole of my school?'

'Er . . . to what might you be referring?' I hedged.

'To the fact that you're bisexual?'

This was news to me. 'Bisexual?! I'm not bisexual . . . I mean, I've got nothing against bisexuals, but I'm not one, or at least not that I'm consciously aware of,' I spluttered. 'Whatever gave them that idea?'

'You did. Apparently that's what you told everyone in your speech yesterday before urging them to celebrate their own bisexuality. Or at least that's what they reckoned you were saying. Apparently you waffled a lot.'

'Aah . . .' I said as the penny began to drop, 'I think these poor benighted young people might have got hold of the wrong end of the stick.'

To add to my mortification, she enlightened me as to the correct word for co-education. It was *coeducación* . . . Who would have thought it?

CHAPTER 2

RICK STEIN AND THE WILD BOARS

What you get when you live out in the sticks, as we do – the only inhabited farm on the east side of the river – is wild animals wandering about the place.

We enjoy and, in certain cases, encourage the presence of wild animals around us. We leave milk thistles to go to seed, for example, because this encourages goldfinches. Ibex, which we see almost every day, are welcome, too; they don't do any damage at all and they are lovely to watch, with their delicate grace and their predilection for posing on the sheerest of pinnacles and crags. Foxes inhabit a grey area, because once a fox has got into your chicken run and massacred your poor hens it's hard to love them. But at times when we do succeed in keeping the hen house foxproof, the fox, too, is a welcome member of the wild.

The sound of foxes barking in the night is a sound of savage yearning melancholy. Of course it drives the dogs, who are not allowed to roam the hills at night, to utter distraction; foxes are what the dogs want to be, and much of their day is spent racing around fruitlessly following the trails of foxes and, occasionally, what they like best of all, finding a particularly ripe dollop of fox shit, and rolling in it. Thus respectably redolent of fox, a smell which is truly loathsome to us humans, they come home and flop down in the house. This is not something we particularly encourage.

I have a firm belief that foxes have a sense of humour, a rare enough thing in an animal. They particularly love to taunt the dogs, and one dark winter night, as Ana and I lolled before the fire flanked by the dozing dogs, a fox had the temerity to walk onto the flat roof and look down at us through the skylight. Bumble and Bao went berserk, rushing about the room, barking and snarling, and fruitlessly leaping at the skylight . . . which didn't do much for our candlelit evening by the fire. The fox considered them for a moment, then turned, calmly shat on the glass, and wandered off.

It's harder to be so sanguine about the wild boar – *jabali* in Spanish, which sounds pleasingly like 'Jabber Lee' – of which there are hundreds living along the river and up in the hills. They, too, are nocturnal creatures, who prefer to hole up in dense thickets during the hours of daylight, though occasionally they misjudge the hour and you come across them trotting home early in the morning. Once, taking Chloé to school in the morning, I saw a mother and no fewer than eight stripy babies. They trotted across the track in an orderly line and disappeared into the thick scrub of oleander and broom on the other side. We felt as if we were on safari.

The wild boars' apparent timidity, however, belies a terrifying ferocity. You don't want to corner a boar, nor find yourself between a female and her babies. They are equipped with terrible tusks and immensely powerful neck and shoulders for delivering the blows. Both males and females are built like battering rams and covered all over with bristles as thick as fencing-wire. And it's no use running; they can run a lot faster than you. Sometimes, walking home late at night, along the track from the bridge to the farm, I hear them snuffling and snorting in the dense scrub beside me. I stop for a moment to listen, and then hasten quietly on.

The boar are multiplying fast in our part of Spain, for they have no predators except the hunters, and most of the hunters who hunt on Campuzano, the hill behind our house, are next to useless. From time to time they organise a Sunday-morning *montería*, where, bristling with guns and arrayed in the very last word in green-drab hunting clobber, dozens of men and scores of dogs bash their way through the scrub on the hills. Sunday morning, though, seems to be a time when the boars are never in. I sometimes come across the hunters on their way back, usually with a tiny dead bird or two swinging from their belts. Archly, I ask these manly men for the boar count, knowing full well that they hardly ever see a boar and almost, but not quite, never bag one.

There's a curious theory linking the fortunes of the wild boar with that of the *butano*, the gas sold throughout Spain in orange steel canisters that almost everybody cooks with. Before the introduction of this gas, found beneath the desert in Algeria, cooking was done on wood fires with fuel bought from *leñeros* – firewood collectors – who would scour the countryside for any combustible material, load it onto their mules and take it to be sold in the towns. The activity of the *leñeros* almost stripped the land bare, leaving very few thickets and wooded *barrancos* – the gullies or gulches where the boar likes to hole up during the day. This lack of cover, along with the scarcity of meat and perhaps the greater skill and courage of earlier, less camouflage-costumed hunters, resulted in a severe reduction in their numbers.

When the gas took over and the *leñeros* were out of a job, the countryside soon returned to its natural wild and overgrown state, a state that the Jabber finds congenial, and the boar population began to rise. At the end of the 1980s, when we arrived at our farm in the Alpujarra, there were hardly any at all, but now the place is seething with them.

The damage they do has to be seen to be believed. A family of boars visiting in the night can dig up a whole field of potatoes or maize. They like to make mudbaths in recently watered earth, too, in which they can roll to ease the terrible burden of fleas with which they are all afflicted. They destroy cultivations, dig up whole plots of vegetables, expose the roots of trees, and the churning of the earth that these activities entail ruins the course of the water across the land, making it impossible to irrigate.

I have a vivid memory of walking down to the river one evening and passing our flock of sheep, who, contented and with full bellies, were lying amongst the long grass and wild flowers in the field by the river. The low evening sun shone from behind, illuminating the outline of each of them in a halo-like blaze of wool; they looked to me like celestial sheep in a paradisaical meadow and I lingered for long minutes, bewitched by the scene. When I returned the next morning the Arcadian idyll had been transformed into something closer to the aftermath of the Somme – the earth churned into formless craters and hills, the grass chomped, shat on and ground into the mud. A few sheep were gingerly picking their way between the ruts and craters. The boar had been in the night.

Wild boar are a menace, the agents of chaos, wrecking the order of things, and their only saving grace is that the younger, tenderer ones are delicious in the pot.

Some years ago, Ana, whose mind is much exercised by strategies to confound the Jabber and keep him out of her vegetable patch, decided to create a hedge of pomegranate, using the tiny plants that come up all over the farm in the autumn. The pomegranate has long thorns, and she figured that the tangled

20

mass of a thorny hedge would be a match even for the bulldozer-like boar. We dug up hundreds of saplings and planted them in a trench along one side of the triangular vegetable patch at the bottom of the farm, then covered them with a line of chicken wire to protect them from the sheep, who would otherwise nibble the young leaves and kill the lot.

Manolo, who helps us labouring on the farm and was in charge of watering this garden, didn't think much of the idea. Manolo is very conservative in a typical Alpujarran way and, if a thing is not traditionally done, it's a hell of a job to get him to accept it and cooperate. He didn't like the pomegranate hedge because such a thing had never been done in the Alpujarra, and he couldn't see the point of it . . . and didn't water it. Pomegranates are pretty drought-resistant, though, so the hedge survived in spite of his constructive neglect; it just took a little longer to get established.

Besides keeping the boar out, the hedge is a delight to look at. In spring it suddenly bursts into life with a sheen of tiny red leaves; in early summer it blossoms into a constellation of dazzling red flowers. Later the fruit comes, perfectly formed but tiny, because of the density of the planting, and then finally in autumn the leaves go from green to yellow to red. I like to trim it with garden shears, as if it were a privet hedge.

Ana views this activity with amusement; she suspects that deep within me lies a conventional suburban man. Still, I've been doing this for a couple of years now, and the hedge is taking on the pleasing form of a green cloud. It's the sort of job you do when you haven't got anything else to do – and, of course, that doesn't happen much. But there was one late summer day when I found myself with a little time to kill while I waited for some visitors, so I took the shears and headed down the hill. It's a long job, because it's a long hedge. I clipped away for the best part of an hour, stepping back from time to time to admire the work and check its progress. As I worked, I thought, among other things, about the boar. There were tracks in the mud beside where I was working, and I wondered how long it would be before they discovered, like a tenacious siege army, some weak chink in the defences and battered their way through.

I was still thinking of this when I heard the horn of a car from the road above the river – we need visitors to announce themselves, so that we can shuttle them up from the river. I downed tools and headed for the bridge. A week earlier I had answered the phone to a man who wondered if we might want to appear on a TV series following the travels of a well-known British chef. I didn't think that we did, really, and was a bit unenthusiastic. But the man on the other end was extremely persuasive and gave me to believe that this would be a very good thing for all parties involved, so I capitulated and suggested that he come and pay us a visit. When I mentioned this to my publishers in London, they positively burbled with excitement. 'It's Rick Stein,

Chris. He's brilliant and has a vast following. Look after these people; give them anything they want.'

There were two men getting out of a car by the bridge when I arrived, a big one and a small one. The bigger one sprang forward, announced himself as David Pritchard, and introduced me to the smaller one, Derek, who was staggering behind him. Poor Derek, who had been driving, was in a bit of a state; in fact, it would not be exaggerating to say that he was unable to speak for a full fifteen minutes. It transpired that he had been absolutely terrified of the road. I shook his limp, quivering hand.

'Well, Chris,' boomed David, who was florid and ebullient and not remotely bothered by the journey. 'I'm dead pleased to meet you and it certainly is a lovely place you've got here. But I have to tell you right now and without further ado that there is no way – absolutely no way – that we can film here. It's just too far, too wild, and the logistical problems of getting the team and all the gear out here would be a nightmare. And what with the budget and the limited time we've got . . . well, it's out of the question . . . we'll have to forget it.'

Derek feebly nodded his heart-felt acquiescence.

'That's OK,' I said, thinking that I had not been the one who had raised the idea in the first place. 'I guess I'll just have to get over it.'

'It's nice here, though. I like it,' David continued. 'And I happen to have a couple of fish with me. Beautiful-looking *sea* bass. I got them from the fish counter in the hypermarket in Motril – one of the

23

best fishmongers I've ever come across. Why don't we go and slap 'em on the grill? Be a shame to waste 'em.'

So we crossed the bridge, poor Derek still shaking, climbed into the farm car, and drove up to the house. David was a man who knew how to do business: as well as a whole heap of fine fish in a bag, he had brought with him a cool-box of Rías Baixas wine. He wormed his way straight to my wife's heart by cunningly contrived commentary upon the plants and being nice to the dogs, and proceeded to prepare us all lunch.

The grilled fish was the star of the show, following a simple starter of hot flatbread and baba ghanoush that we had knocked up earlier, alluringly sprinkled with pomegranate seeds. David was a gifted cook – more of the rumbustuous than the delicate school – and, jollied along by the wine, we enjoyed a long, lingering and rather noisy lunch. Even Derek temporarily forgot the terrors of the morning. As the afternoon drew to a close, we all vowed eternal friendship and lamented long and bitterly the fact that the part we would have had to play in the cookery programme was not to be.

'But I love this place, I always have done,' insisted David, a little crapulously, 'and I know my man would love it, too. He's read all your books and he just loves 'em – crazy about 'em, in fact. He'll be gutted that we can't film here. It's a crying shame but it can't be helped; there's no way I can get the crew out here, no way at all.' Derek, who was sinking into an anxious gloom at the thought of the journey home, roused himself briefly to nod at this.

It was about three days later when the phone rang again. 'Chris, it's David. I been thinking about your place ever since that lunch, and I've come to the conclusion that we've got to do it. My man would never forgive me if we don't. It'll be the best part of the show. I know I said it couldn't be done, but I reckon it can. Can you give us a couple of options for next month?'

And thus it was that I embarked upon yet another career, mercifully short this time, as a guest television cook.

What, I wondered, ought one to make for the delectation of Rick, not to mention the foodies who would be watching? Some ecological dish perhaps, composed of our own home-grown ingredients and cooked in a sustainable way, using almond shells and dried rosemary. Fish was the thing of David's man, but fish is one of the things that don't grow on the farm. I crossed fish off the list.

Over the coming weeks I tried various things out on Ana and Chloé, many of them heavily loaded in favour of the cucumber, for we were suffering from a glut of cucumbers that year. But you can only eat so many cucumber dishes, and we were pushing the limits: cucumber soup, cucumber sorbet, cucumbers fried, curried, baked and stuffed, even a detestable cucumber lemonade. But, as Ana pointed out, the viewers were hardly going to make a big effort to tune in to find out how to cook a cucumber.

I abandoned the cucumber and cast about for something a bit sexier and more televisual. The pomegranate is of course about as televisual as a thing can be, but there's only so much you can do with one, beyond eating its seeds. Pomegranate syrup is good, but the preparation of it makes for rather tedious viewing.

Then, a week before we were due to receive David and his man, the hunters rang me to say that there was to be a *montería* that Sunday morning, and that we ought to keep the sheep shut in the stable because of the risk from the hunting dogs that they always, without fail, seem to leave behind them. Just a few hours later, they rang again, bubbling with manly pride, to say that, through some bizarre circumstances, they had actually managed to find a boar and shoot it, and that if I wanted some I could go up and collect it.

My heart went out first to the ill-starred boar, who had so badly misjudged his Saturday-night ramble as to be discovered on the hill on the Sunday morning, and then it occurred to me: of course, boar. There would be a deliciously appropriate irony in cooking one up on the telly. What a way to get my own back for the years of ravages that we had suffered at the hands – or, more accurately, the snouts – of the boar population. Accordingly, I set off up the hill to fetch the main ingredient in a dish that was already taking shape in my mind.

It took about forty-five minutes to find the hunters. There were two of them, a beefy young lad and a tough wiry man, both wearing hunters' garb and forage hats. Neither of them were friendly; this was manly business. We roped the dead beast up, and set off through the rosemary, taking up the strain to drag it behind us. It stayed exactly where it was. We took a breather and tried again but still it resisted the combined might of the three of us; boars are heavy creatures, and this was a big one. There was no way we could move it, so the thin man took out his hunting knife and set about dismembering it. With considerable skill, and a knife that was heavy as an axe and razor-sharp, he took off the head, flayed the bristly skin from the flesh, and cut the rest of it into two halves.

These we hoisted onto our shoulders, slimy with blood and wobbling with fat, and started through the thick undergrowth down the hill.

The lad carried the head – which was no mean feat, as it was slippery with congealing blood and must have weighed the best part of twenty kilos – while the military-looking man and me carried a side each, and the sides weighed even more. The pair of them were young and very fit and I hobbled and stumbled to keep up with them, making constant adjustments to the gruesome load that slipped and slid constantly from my grip. Eventually, casting squeamishness aside, I carried it over my head, my hair now caked in gore and grease. The viewers would not want to see this aspect of the meal, I thought to myself, as I staggered and twisted my knee a little.

I hung that side of boar in the old kitchen, where there were fewer flies than in the stable. The hunters promised to ring me when they had the results of the trichinosis test, certifying its safety, and departed.

You have to be cautious with eating wild boar, and a sample of meat must be examined under a microscope to establish that it is free from disease. Everyone has to do this as a matter of routine. And, of course, it wouldn't do to kill a TV chef. Fortunately the result came through as negative, so I butchered the meat and froze it, leaving enough out for a substantial stew for Mr Stein.

The big day came. I had prepared the stew of boar the night before. Stews, as I'm sure you know, get better and better by the day, and I figured that, with all the other stuff that would be going down on the morrow, it would be advisable to have at least a part of the job already done. This is what I did: first of all I browned those chunks of boar. I zapped them in hot, hot oil so they seared in a matter of seconds. This, the searing, is one of the important things to get right for the success of your stew. After the first batch is browned, you need to tip away the liquid that has gathered in the pan, and start again; otherwise, the next batch will be boiled rather than seared . . . and boiled boar is what you don't want. If you want to use those juices later, which is no bad thing, you can add them to the onions once you have zapped them in a little oil after the meat.

I took the meat out of the pan and added a load of sliced onions, a heap of garlic, a couple of red-hot headbanger chillies and some bay leaves, all from the garden. Then there was half a bush of rosemary from the hill and the grated peel of a few oranges and lemons. Once this lot was fizzing away nicely, I tipped in the seared meat, and a couple of tins of tomatoes, fresh from the larder . . . I know there were tomatoes in the garden, but it saves a lot of messing about taking the skins off and, besides, tinned tomatoes are delicious at any time of the year. And finally a tin of tomato puree, and a couple of squares of black chocolate . . . not for pudding, but for that nice thick black slimy Mexican texture. Hell of a stew, I thought to myself as I sucked the wooden spoon.

Russell, our English neighbour from La Herradura, the next farm down the river, had been wheedled into bringing the crew across the river and up to the farm in his Range Rover. It was a rough old Range Rover, but I think he had been up half the night polishing it and mucking out its typical farm car interior.

In a flurry of dust the car rolled up beneath the house and Rick Stein and the crew disembarked. We all shook hands and said how pleased we were to meet one another, and without further ado David swung into action.

'Russell, take Rick back down the hill and drive

up again. Rick, you get out of the car and come up to the steps where you shake hands with Chris and Ana. Got it? Off you go.'

Russell and Rick backed down the drive while David pushed us into position.

'Right. When Rick comes up, you go down the steps and act like this is the first time you've ever met. OK?'

The sun shone; Russell drove up again; Rick got out; the dogs barked; Ana and I sashayed down the steps; we all oozed inane enthusiasm and bonhomie; Rick said again that he was really pleased to meet us and handed us an enormous string of garlic in a purple fishnet bag; Ana and I reached out together to grab it . . .

'CUT! Hold it there. Only one of you wants to go for the garlic. You look like you've never seen a string of garlic in your lives. We'll do it again. Russell, back down the hill. Ana, Chris, back up the steps.'

Rick clambered back into the car clutching the garlic and Russell backed off down the hill again. Ana and I and Bumble and Bao bounced back up the steps. Once again, Russell drove up; the dogs barked; the door opened and out rolled the string of garlic. 'CUT! One more time, please. Hang on to that garlic will you, Rick.'

I muttered to Ana that I thought the string of garlic was a bit of a crap present. After all, we grew our own garlic; we had heaps of it. 'Yes, but he doesn't know us, does he? And don't be ungracious; it's very nice of him.'

'QUIET! Back down the hill, Russell, Rick. Ana, Chris, back up the steps . . . Go!'

We went back up the steps, followed by the dogs, who were starting to get confused. Rick got in the car again; Russell rolled backwards.

'Let's see if we can't get it right this time,' said David.

Up came Russell in the car; Rick got out, clutching the garlic; the dogs looked on in silence; Rick said yet again that he was really pleased to meet us; we all looked at one another for a bit. 'The garlic, Rick. Hand over the garlic,' admonished David. 'Hallo, Rick,' I said. 'I've heard a lot about you.' I held out my hand to shake, but Rick was still proffering the garlic. I shook the garlic . . . 'CUT!'

Down the hill went Russell and Rick. Ana and I went back up the steps with the dogs, me holding the garlic. 'Chris, give the garlic back to Rick, will you?'

Followed by the dogs, I walked down the track to where Russell and Rick were waiting for the signal, and handed over the garlic. Rick grinned at me wanly.

'One more time. Everybody ready? Roll.'

Finally we got it nearly right. It went something like this: Russell and Rick arrived; the dogs barked; Ana and I walked down the steps; Rick got out of the car with the garlic, and said goodbye to Russell; Rick said for the fifth or sixth time how pleased he was to meet us and handed the garlic to Ana, who received it graciously; we all shook hands and

I said, 'Rick Steen, good to meet you; I've heard a lot about you.'

'It's Stein, Chris. Rick Stein, not Rick Steen,' said David. 'We'll do it one last time.'

And so we did and this time we got it, as I think one says in the film world, in the can.

As you may imagine, we were all feeling a little tired after completing this scene, and we had hardly started the session yet. There was considerable scope for more cock-ups, I thought, when we got onto the real business. But for now what was needed was a little alcohol. We served some beers and wines and offered around some roasted almonds and capers and pots of home-grown olives, *Arbequinas* and *Acebuches*, which we reckoned Rick would not have come across before – they're tiny with very little flesh, and most people would think that they're not worth the trouble, but take it from me, they are.

The load lightened and we all had a giggle about what had just happened, and started to get to know one another a little. I had boned up enough on Rick's work to know he was a man after my own heart when it came to sustainable fishing and the rustling up of food, but he was an easy guest too, unassuming and with a ready charm. The cameraman and sound recordist wandered about the place getting what they called 'atmospheric stuff', while the rest of us got into the mood for cookery. I slipped on a clean apron and with a whetstone whipped up an edge on some knives. Ana went down to the vegetable garden with Rick and the camera to get some home-grown vegetable shots.

The meal plan was as follows: we would start with some lightly fried lambs' balls, dusted with beaten egg and breadcrumbs, and fried in oil and butter with a hint of chilli and thyme. You don't often get lambs' balls in Britain, so I figured that this would be a rare treat for the visitors. A tabouleh would be next, a mountain of mint and parsley chopped up with tomatoes, chilli and ginger and bulghur wheat, lemon juice, and perhaps a small red onion finely chopped and soaked for half an hour in icy water to take the worst of the kick out of it. If anybody fancied it, there would be some yoghurt with garlic, chilli (I put chilli in everything, as a consequence of having once visited Mexico), ginger and fresh coriander, to slop on the tabouleh.

Then would come the pièce de résistance, the thick red meaty stew accompanied by the lightest creamiest *aligote* – mashed potato with cheese and garlic – and finally, to dazzle the senses, Ana's floral salad, one of the most beautiful dishes that ever graced a table. It would certainly look good on the telly, we thought.

We all repaired to the kitchen to get this stuff on the move. Amid the clashing of knives and the bubbling and steaming of pots, I liberally bestowed cookery hints upon the patient Rick, who did his level best to assume an amused interest. I told him for example, that I thought people were far too fussy about food hygiene and, as a species, it was not doing us any good. 'You've got to eat a peck of dirt before you die,' I ranted. 'What possible harm can come from a handful of blue-bottles on your meat? If meat is dangerously off, the smell is so bad you can't get near it . . .' and other singular and questionable pronouncements. 'Lemon squeezers are for pussycats,' I told him, squeezing a lemon through my hand and filtering the pips with my fingers. I think he took note of this particular hint for future use.

By this time, what with all the dithering about that is the inevitable concomitant of filming, we were all starting to feel just a little bit hungry. All the talk of food and the kitchen badinage did nothing to allay this. Ana and Rick sat down at the table and I burst through the fly curtain with a pan full of hot balls. There were just the three of us eating and it was hardly the most relaxed meal I have had in my life, as there was a big fluffy sock of a microphone dangling over the table and the long snout of a camera sticking into my left ear. The hunger getting a grip now, I sat up in my chair and raised a glass of wine to my wife and the guests, and then, fairly quivering with antici-pation, I speared a hot ball with my fork and raised it to my lips.

'CUT!' cried David.

CHAPTER 3

THE GREEN, GREEN ROOVES
OF HOME

Few people get to see their homes from above. We have that pleasure from not just one but two vantage points: one on the mountain path that leads up to what used to be a threshing floor, the other from the opposite side of the valley where a lone almond tree marks a bend in the track. The latter is the spot that I ask visitors to look out for, because if you honk your horn as you pass this tree the acoustics carry the sound all the way across the valley to the ears of the dogs. The dogs start barking, which wakes me from whatever reverie I am indulging, and leaves me just enough time to hare down the hill and meet the approaching vehicle at our bridge (as I had with David before that first fish lunch).

From either of these points you can make out the peculiar agglomeration that we call home: a muddle of more or less rectangular stone boxes emerging from a rocky hillside, half hidden by a riot of jacaranda, morning glory, wisteria and jasmine. Below, you can make out a path winding down through terraces of oranges and lemons to

36

the sheep stable and a hillock known as La Haza de la Cruz – 'the meadow of the cross' – which presides over the confluence of two rivers, the Cádiar and the Trevélez.

There's something deeply gratifying about looking down on a house that you yourself have built, but what makes it even better is the innovation we've recently added to our otherwise traditional home and outhouses – the 'green rooves' of El Valero. These give the pleasing impression of tiny terraces of grass, hovering beside the outhouses, and after the spring rains have done their best the foliage on the roof becomes so thick that parts of the house seem to disappear entirely.

I sometimes wonder about our house and the building of it and our offbeat ideas. After all, what initially attracted me to the Alpujarra was the simplicity and honesty of the architecture, the attempts by the rural poor to create a little beauty with whatever lay to hand. The perfect proportions of a handsome hen house; an oil-drum set on a plinth of stone, painted white and planted with yellow and white flowers; a stone wall moulded to fit the leaning trunk of an olive tree: these were the delights that won my heart. From the point of view of authenticity I fear we may be running the risk of killing the thing we love.

On the other hand, one has to move forward, take advantage of new developments. Had we not done so we might still be living in architecturally honest turf huts, smoked half to death by peat fires. And the changes we were making, while they gladdened our hearts with their beauty, were fairly unostentatious and, of course, sustainable. Our home is powered entirely by solar panels, which, arrayed upon the rooves, glint royal blue in the sunshine; we keep warm in winter by burning wood that we grow on the farm or gather from the river; kitchen and bathroom water is used for irrigation, and all the leftovers are either composted or made into edible eggs by the hens. All in all, it makes us feel pretty good about our impact on the earth in general and on the Alpujarra in particular.

The desire to add beauty to building is not universal in the Alpujarra, where function and cost is king. Witness my neighbour, Domingo, a sheep farmer and nurseryman. For the last fifteen years he has been living with Antonia, a Dutch sculptor who moved to the valley in search of inspiration and then found it in . . . well, him. By some sort of osmosis he developed his own hitherto latent artistic talents to the point that he, too, has become a sculptor of some renown. Yet Domingo thinks nothing of artlessly incorporating rusty old bulldozer parts into his studio, an old car seat for those rare moments of repose, a cracked wing mirror for shaving. And then there's Bernardo, who seems blissfully unaware of any aesthetic paradox in hanging a dead goat in the shower to keep off the flies.

However, by odd chance, we happened upon two like-minded souls, a handsome young couple called Simon and Victoria, who not only shared our aesthetic vision of optimising the simple beauty of the landscape but carried it several steps further. They had just married when they arrived in our lives, and were on honeymoon, having chosen rather unaccountably to spend it camping in the desert of Almería. On one night and one night only in the last thousand years has it snowed in the desert of Almería, and it happened to be the very night that Simon and Vicky pitched their tent. The snow flurried in, driven by a howling gale through the flaps of their flimsy tent, nearly freezing them to death. The next night they put up at a little hotel in the High Alpujarra, in Bérchules. In their room was a guidebook with an advertisement for our holiday cottage. It was the only advertisement in the book and, curiously enough, in about five years Simon and Victoria were the only people who ever replied to it.

So they came to stay for a few days to thaw out and, in the inevitable way of these things, ended up living with us for eighteen months. They were the perfect guests: we adored them and they seemed to like us too, and we all became part of each other's family. They had an unconventional way of making a living: they were designers and constructors of aquariums – not little fish tanks but colossal municipal affairs full of sharks and rays and barracuda and sunfish. The business of building aquariums is somewhat unpredictable and you are often left hanging on for months while the promoters in various parts of the world get the finance together. Which accounted for them having the time to live with us.

Simon is a brilliant draughtsman, designer and constructor, and always has to have some project to amuse him. One day, about a month into their stay, he sidled up to me when Ana was out of hearing. 'Have you ever given any thought to the idea of green rooves for El Valero?' he asked.

'Scarcely a day passes, Simon, scarcely a day. Tell me more.' I was all ears, and for an hour or more we retired into deep confabulation. Occasionally Ana would appear, and we would fall into an unnatural silence, or pretend to be talking about something that we were not really talking about at all.

A recent plan I had devised for building a new bathroom out of straw bales had come adrift after Ana discovered it meant knocking a great hole in our existing bathroom wall. She and Chloé had taken exception to the idea that passing strangers might take advantage and wander in. I feared that the grass roof idea might fall on similarly stony ground, so to speak, but in fact I needn't have worried. What Ana likes best, apart from animals – and perhaps Chloé and me – is plants, and so she found the idea of a carpet of plants providing insulation for the house pretty appealing.

Simon's green roof seemed a logical step for us.

Already the walls of the house are so covered in ivy and wisteria that the sun barely touches them at all in summer, and this makes a spectacular difference to the temperature inside the house. With an extra layer of vegetation on the roof, we would be cool in summer and warm in winter – as cucumbers and toast – for no running cost at all. These, too, were powerful considerations for Ana.

The dyed-in-the-wool Manolo took a little more convincing. When we broke the news to him, he grinned his broadest grin and looked from Ana to me and then back to Ana, waiting to see who would crack first and admit that we were 'taking his hair', as the Spanish have it. 'You want to put grass on the roof?' he repeated incredulously and waited. 'You mean grass . . . on the roof?', he tried again, but still we simply agreed that this was indeed the plan. For days he continued his bewildered refrain of 'Grass . . . on the roof?', breaking off into a chuckle and shake of the head. I've no doubt that in the ensuing weeks he drummed up free drinks from Tíjola to Órgiva using just those four hilarious words.

Eager to proceed, we pored over the Internet for details. In Tokyo, Osaka and Kuala Lumpur green rooves were quite the thing, but it turned out that Freiburg in Germany had the most advanced projects, so much of our information came from there and little by little our plans took root.

The first thing we had to do was to properly waterproof and reinforce all the rooves in question by covering them in a layer of steel-mesh-reinforced concrete, then a welded layer of PVC. This detracted somewhat from our green credentials, as PVC is hardly an ecologically sound material, but one must be pragmatic. On top of the PVC went another layer of waterproof concrete, then a special felt, like old army blankets, and on top of all that a layer that looked like plastic eggboxes. These held water for a good long period of time. The eggboxes were covered with fine filter cloth and then a deep layer of soil mixed with balls of *arlita*. Simon said the soil should be as inert as possible, for some reason which still escapes me.

Arlita is exploded balls of clay, like Sugar Puffs: they're water-retentive and excellent for growing plants, but their main advantage is that they lighten the load. With unadulterated soil you run the risk, when it rains, of the roof becoming waterlogged, the weight being too much for the supporting beams, and the whole shebang crashing into the room below.

The *arlita* came all the way from Barcelona in enormous sacks on the back of a truck and Domingo came down to the river to ferry the sacks across on his tractor. It was clear that he was interested – anything remotely innovative piques his curiosity, but he usually prefers not to show it. That day, however, he asked me a few laconic questions about the project, which for him is akin to wild enthusiasm.

Clearly something was up, but he waited until

we had loaded the last batch to fill me in. 'The papers came through from Madrid yesterday. I've bought the farm,' he said.

It was a simple enough sentence and delivered in the same manner that one might announce the purchase of a new pig. I looked at Domingo, my mouth open in amazement while he grinned sheepishly and traced a pattern in the dirt with the toe of his shoe. 'Domingo! I had no idea,' I cried. '¡Enhorabuena! Congratulations, I'm delighted.'

And I was. For Domingo was the only farmer in the valley who hadn't – until this moment – owned his own land, and he was without doubt the most passionate lover of the land. Both he and his father before him had rented their farm for a peppercorn rent from landowners in Madrid who had never even seen the place. For many years he had been trying to negotiate to buy the farm off them, with absolutely no success, but finally he had done it. It was impossible to overestimate just how much a thing like this meant. Country people have an insatiable hunger for land; now at last Domingo could put into practice his own projects for improving his home and the land that surrounded it. I grabbed him and gave him a hug. Someone needed to be emotional about this extraordinary event, and it certainly wasn't going to be Domingo himself.

The fact that Domingo hadn't actually derided our scheme with the green rooves, and had even lent a hand with the *arlita*, brought a change of heart in Manolo, who soon made tentative comments that he thought the scheme, though harebrained, might just stand a chance of success.

The insulation and waterproofing layers were complete. Now it was time to plant the roof with drought- and heat-resistant plants. This was Ana's scheme and was inspired by her finding a spectacularly beautiful succulent in the semi-desert of Almería. How any plant could survive such conditions seemed little short of miraculous. Ana identified it as a *Sedum* and set about rooting scores of cuttings in her nursery. She then cast about for other plants that might thrive in the taxing conditions of a flat roof in the Andalucian summer. They included *Mesembrianthemum*, *Carpobrotus*, *Crassula* and a whole lot of others that I still don't know the names of.

Now that the roof is established, lavender, several thymes and alyssum have sown themselves in profusion, and the aerial view of our house has taken on the look of a rather scruffy hanging garden, particularly now that I have sown the roof of the *cámara*, the annexe where we keep our library, with wheat, barley and poppies.

The green roof is a thing of great beauty and, because we had Simon as master of the works, it is also professionally done and ought to last us a lifetime. As a consequence we now have one of the very few rooves in the Alpujarra that does not leak when it rains. This is a terrific advantage, and it really does have the effect of keeping the interior of the house cooler in summer and warmer in winter. As Manolo is fond of pointing out to all-comers, *'El techo verde es lo suyo'* – 'A green roof is the way to go.'

CHAPTER 4

HOW EL VALERO GOT ITS NAME

One of the key principles of country living is always to have time for one's neighbours . . . though it's not always an easy one to follow. One day recently I was hurtling out of the valley, late for an appointment with the dentist. Antonio, Domingo's cousin, was sauntering down the track and signalled me to stop. I wound down the window and he leaned on it, idly flipping the long end of his horse's leading rope and grinning. It was one of those grins with a little more depth and complexity than his everyday grin; there was purpose of some sort behind it.

'We could do with a little rain,' I offered, non-committally.

'No, no, no, it's fine. Plenty of grazing still. You'll be OK over at El Valero, anyway . . .'

He seemed to be pacing out some sort of a conversational treasure map, unsure of which line to follow. He continued: 'I'll tell you why El Valero got its name . . .'

Lawd, I thought. I've lived here for God knows how many years now and I'm late for the dentist, and he goes and chooses this moment to tell me how my farm got its name.

'It's got to do with grazing, you know, *vale – valero*. The grazing's good, even in a dry year . . . Ah, and you know that mule of Juan's?' He had found whatever it was he had been looking for and slipped into gear.

'Which Juan?'

'You know Juan Gomarota, the big one . . .' (*Gomarota* means 'broken rubber' and is Juan's slightly cruel *apodo* or nickname).

'Ah, *that* Juan . . . I didn't know he had a mule.'

'He doesn't, but he did once. Anyway, that mule was a hell of a worker. It used to belong to a shepherd who rented the grazing at El Valero one winter. There was nothing for the sheep to eat anywhere – you think you've seen dry, well, this is nothing. He had three hundred and fifty sheep and they were thin as pencils, hungry like snails on a mirror; they were in a terrible state. So in that dry, dry winter he brought his whole flock to El Valero for the grazing. There's always *retama* and *albaida* and *romero* there (broom, anthyllis and rosemary) Anyway, the flock recovered, and in a short time they were fat as butter, and the grazing lasted them all year. It's good, your hill. Thus the name: El Valero.'

He had got this wrong actually. I had often wondered about the farm's name but so far as I could discover, it doesn't mean anything. It's Campuzano, the hill on whose slope our farm lies, that is named for the quality of its grazing: *campo sano* – healthy land.

I slipped the clutch an inch, to make the car lurch towards the waiting dentist.

Antonio wasn't having it, though. He was in full flow now. 'Anyway,' he continued, hanging on imperviously to the lurching car. 'The shepherd had two boys and they were wild, and one of them had a bicycle . . .'

'Aah,' I interjected. I'm not good at letting people get on with monologues uninterrupted, and I felt that the various 'hmms' that I'd so far offered were not sufficiently encouraging – although the last thing I wanted to do was to encourage him. I wanted to get to the dentist; I hadn't been for nine years and I had a throbbing tooth. But the bicycle was a good touch, an unexpected narrative element. There never have been many bicycles in the Alpujarra – it's not bicycling country, and also the nature of the indigenes is such that a bicycle would have been considered a rather racy and even improper thing. I put the handbrake on.

'What they did was tie the bicycle to the mule's tail and in this way they rode all over the Alpujarras, one on the mule and one on the bike. Of course, their father gave them a belting when he found out, but they had a lot of fun in the meantime. When they sold the mule, Fat Juan bought it. He said it was great to work with, except that it went berserk at the sight of a wheelbarrow or a concrete mixer.'

I said that I didn't believe they had actually tied

a concrete mixer to its tail. 'No,' said Antonio. 'But a concrete mixer has a wheel and I suppose in the eyes of a mule that makes it similar to a bicycle.'

As a story the whole thing wasn't up to much. I've heard worse, but on a scale of one to ten I'd give it two, or perhaps three. And these days I get told a lot of stories. The locals know that I write books about the Alpujarras, and the notion of having your story written down seems to exercise a peculiar appeal. They don't seem to expect any reward but, of course, the stories aren't always good ones, and they are not always told when you want to hear them.

Indeed, I had no sooner managed to shake Antonio off and was racing toward the town, driving like a banshee with the toothache, when just past the banana grove at El Granadino my old friend José Parra – a man who, rather oddly, keeps a lorry in his front room – leapt out into the road before me.

'Cristóbal, *qué tal*? Hey, I've got something to tell you . . .'

I looked pointedly at my watch. José Parra looked as if whatever he was about to tell me had been carefully rehearsed. 'You know there used to be a mill up the river beyond your place . . .'

I arrived an hour late for the dentist, which, as it happened, was no bad thing, as he too was behind, so I only had to wait another twenty minutes.

★   ★   ★

Occasionally, though in truth not often, someone will tell me a story that etches itself deep into my mind and either illuminates or throws long shadows over the place I call home. Such a story was told to me by Rogelio, a sheep farmer who lives up on Cerro Negro, the Black Hill.

Rogelio is the mildest of men, with white hair and apple cheeks and his farm is a fine example of how an Alpujarran farm ought to be run: the trees are all neatly pruned with an axe, and at their feet are stacked little piles of firewood; runnels and rills of clear water burble along earth channels and cascade over stone walls even to the far corner of the most distant terrace. Well-tended crops delight the critical eye. It speaks of hard work, a deep love of the land, and plenty of good home produce.

I have known him for years, for he had a little flock of sheep that I used to shear and, although it barely repaid the cost of the petrol to drive up to his farm, I relished the few afternoons we spent together. Inevitably the day arrived when I had to announce that I was hanging up my shears and would no longer be able to shear the flock. He took this stoically and, after I had finished, invited me to watch the sun dropping low on the Contraviesa and share a few glasses of rough country wine. We had been sitting for a while in contemplative silence when I asked him if he had always lived at La Palma, his *cortijo*.

'No,' he replied. 'I bought this farm forty-five years ago for five thousand pesetas. I was born way over there,' and he indicated the great range of rolling blue hills that we were overlooking down to the south. 'We lived in a very remote spot, just the three of us, my brother my mother and me.'

'And your father?'

'My father died before I was old enough to know him. As I said, there were just the three of us, and we had no other family anywhere near. I say no family; we didn't even have any neighbours, it was that far out. Then, when I was eight years old, my brother ten, our mother fell ill and went to a hospital in Granada. The doctors told her that she would not leave there and would die there very soon. Her last wish was to see her sons before she died, so somehow she managed to find a taxi driver to come to the Contraviesa and take us back with him to Granada. Somehow he managed to find us and took us away with him to the hospital. When we arrived in the city – and we had never been in a city before – our mother was already dead. The taxi driver told us we owed him eight thousand pesetas.'

'Eight thousand pesetas,' I cried. 'But that's more than you paid for this farm.'

'That's what he said we owed him, eight thousand pesetas. How were my brother and I to know what this meant? We were children, and had never earned so much as a single peseta in all our lives.'

'But the man was a monster, to take such cruel advantage of a couple of children . . . and children who had just lost their mother. I can't believe that anybody could be so vicious.'

'Well,' said Rogelio quietly, 'That was what this man wanted, and my brother and I vowed that we would pay him every peseta of what we owed him . . . and we did.'

He looked up and smiled in the gentle way he had. I wanted to weep. I thought of those two children alone in the world and walking from Granada back to the Contraviesa; it would have taken them two or three days probably, with no money, no food. And I thought of the monstrous heartlessness of the taxi driver. And then I looked at Rogelio; he was trimming with a razor-sharp knife, a handle for his axe. He bore no rancour, was not eaten to his soul with desire for vengeance against this appalling injustice. This gentle and unassuming countryman had come through a most terrible trial, a trial that would have destroyed most men by twisting their hearts with bitterness. It's surprising where one finds such deep wells of strength and courage.

'So how did you pay off the debt?'

'We worked at whatever we could find for years and years, keeping nothing for ourselves, until it was finally paid.'

After he had told me the story, I drove back down the hill to the river. The very landscape looked different; I could hardly help super-imposing upon it the recent past with its poverty, its cruelty and its misery . . . and the glorious counterpoint to all those evils, that makes us what we are: strength, generosity of spirit, joyfulness, goodness. In South America they have a saying, which I fear they have often needed to see them through the long years of misery: '*Los buenos, somos más*' – 'The good, there are more of us.'

For a long time afterwards I would mull over this story of Rogelio's. It moved me deeply, but I found that whenever I tried to relate it to others great gaps seemed to appear in the narrative begging to be filled. How had the children managed to find their way home? How had they not only supported themselves but managed to pay off such a huge debt? No doubt Rogelio had told me but I had failed, as a result of my shaky language skills and sieve-like memory, to note them. There was also the problem that I was, and always have been, a rather passive listener. I have none of that editorial acuteness that good interviewers have, who can distance themselves enough to lob in a note of enquiry.

The more I thought about it, the more convinced I became that I should revisit this story with Rogelio. In fact, the episode had revived a dormant but cherished ambition that I had nurtured long before I'd written any stories of my own: to collect the tales told by the old folk about life on the mountain farms when they were teeming with people. I used fondly to imagine myself trudging the rocky ways of the Alpujarra (an activity like this ought to be done on foot to give it respectability and authenticity) armed with pen and notebook and perhaps a tiny, unobtrusive tape recorder. I would seek out the old folks with stories to tell, and they, bent over their mattocks, or leaning on the bar in remote village taverns, would share with me their stories of the past. Anthropological ethnography, I think the term is. Now, with the passing of the years, the old ambition had taken on a new urgency. The old folk, many of them left as the sole original occupants of mountain villages or near-derelict farms, were disappearing fast, and with it my chance to offer this community some writing of lasting cultural value.

My mind was set. But, as so often happens, other more pressing tasks intervened and I found myself delaying and then delaying again the launch of my grand project and, as I was no longer shearing, I had no other reason to go up to Cerro Negro. I didn't see Rogelio for a long time. And then, one day, not long after the hunters had slain the boar, our dogs, Bumble and Bao, decided to head off into the hills on their own and disappeared.

I had made myself hoarse from shouting their names, and was pretty fed up with searching, when an Englishwoman who lived up on Cerro Negro rang to say that Ana was lying beneath the shade of a hedge in her garden and could I go and fetch her. Having established that she was talking not about my wife but one of our dogs (who have collars with the name 'Ana' and our telephone number), I set out, initially irked by having this long errand. Then I realized that the hedge in question was not far from Rogelio's farm. This was too good an opportunity. I would visit him and flesh out the story I had begun. I printed it out and, armed with a brand-new pen and notebook, and a dog-lead, set off.

Parking on the edge of the track up on Cerro Negro, I set out on foot for the final stretch to Rogelio's farm. Save the distant drone of a brush-cutter and the sound of goat bells coming up from the valley, it was quiet up there, far from the constant rushing of the rivers. A few flies kept me company. I pulled the brim of my hat down to keep off the glare of the midday sun.

I called out loudly as I approached the house, this being the accepted etiquette for approaching an isolated *cortijo*. Shortly Rogelio emerged from round the corner of the house, holding an armful of laundry and a bag of clothes pegs. His wife was having trouble with her legs, apparently, and was bedridden, so Rogelio was now her full-time carer, and did all the housework as well as tending the farm. All this at eighty-two, and at harvest time he was still climbing high into the big old olive trees to beat down those last reluctant olives. He told me that he had picked over three tons by himself the previous winter. With a big smile he showed me the peg bag, which had a rather pretty doll's dress sewn up at the bottom and a coathanger fixed to the top, so you could hang it on the line while you worked. It was an unexpected little masterpiece of intermediate technology, and typical of the witty and ingenious shifts of the rural poor of the Alpujarras and no doubt the rest of the country, too.

'Cristóbal,' he said, turning to me with a weather-beaten smile. 'It's good to see you, but what brings you all the way up here. It can't be to waste your time talking to an old man like me, surely?'

'But it is, Rogelio. It is. You remember that story you told me when I was last here, the one about your mother's last days and the great debt you had to repay?'

'I do,' he said, with a peg in his mouth, as he skilfully smoothed the creases from the crumpled dress.

'Well, I think it's such a wonderful story that I would like to write it down and perhaps include it in a book with other stories like it, and I wanted to ask you if you would have any objections?'

'Why would I object, Cristóbal? So long as I don't come out of it too badly, as a villain for example, or a snake . . .'

'Oh, no, no, of course not, Rogelio; in fact you come out of it rather as a hero. I've already written it down and I think I've painted a rather nice portrait of you . . . and a true one. But I'd like to clarify a few details. Would it be OK if I ask you some questions and write down the answers?'

'Why, of course, Cristóbal. I have nothing in particular to do and nowhere to be going, so why don't we do it right now? You're very welcome.'

This is what I love about people like Rogelio: they're positive, agreeable and easy; nothing's a

56

problem. He beckoned me over to a couple of low, rush-seated chairs in the deep green shade of a carob tree. We talked for a time of cooking – Rogelio, unfashionably, likes his food very well done, more or less carbonised – then of washing machines and their various merits and defects, then of the electricity that powers them, then we moved on to a critical appraisal of a vintage bulldozer that his neighbour had just been cornered into buying. I was itching to get down to the nub of the business, but it doesn't do to be too hasty: one must deal with the social niceties first. Well, the social niceties kept us at it for the best part of forty-five minutes until finally I reached into my bag and drew out the printed pages.

'Let me read you what I already wrote. You'll see that you come out of it pretty well.'

Rogelio turned in his chair and leaned forward on his stick to listen. I unfolded the paper and started to translate. He nodded his head with a smile at the mention of the five thousand pesetas that his farm had cost him.

I read on: 'We lived in a very remote spot, just the three of us, my mother my brother and me . . .'

'That's wrong,' he interjected. 'We were five children; my eldest sister was seventeen when our mother died.'

'Er . . . oh, er, that rather changes things. I thought you said you only had one brother.' I was a bit shaken by this revelation that I had got one of the most fundamental aspects of the story completely wrong. Could my Spanish really have been so bad when I first heard this tale? Still, it was a terrific story, and perhaps it could still be retrieved.

I continued reading: 'We didn't even have any neighbours; it was that far out . . .'

'No, it wasn't,' interrupted Rogelio. 'We lived on the edge of the village; there were lots of neighbours.'

I stopped and looked up at him. The carpet was being pulled out from under my feet. The wonderful story that I had cherished for so long was slowly falling to pieces. If there were neighbours, then the drama and pathos of the story would be considerably diminished. I started to feel a little dejected. How could I have got these things wrong?

A little less confidently now, I read on: 'The doctors told my mother that she would not leave the hospital but would die there very soon. Her last wish was to see her sons before she died . . .'

'No,' said Rogelio. 'We never went to Granada. We never saw our mother alive again after she went to the city.'

I lowered the printed pages, and stared at him. 'And the business with the taxi driver . . . and the eight thousand pesetas that you spent your whole childhood repaying? What about that?'

'What taxi driver?'

I was clutching at straws now: 'The taxi driver who took you to Granada to visit your mother in hospital . . .'

'I just told you: we never went to Granada. As for the eight thousand pesetas, well, yes, after my mother's death we owed eight thousand pesetas, to people who had lent us money or helped us out . . . and we vowed to pay every last *duro* of it. In fact, we paid it all off within the year. It was a hell of a good year and we had a terrific harvest of figs.'

Well, I'll tell you now that I was mighty pleased that things had turned out so well for Rogelio and his siblings in the end, but there was a disconsolate feeling welling up in me too, at the utter rubbishing of my cherished tale. I think I must have let the disappointment show in my face.

'During the war the soldiers shot our dog,' said Rogelio, as if in recompense for my lost tale. 'And it was a really good dog, too. But they shot everybody's dogs so they wouldn't give them away by barking.'

This was scant comfort, to say the least. How could I have made such a hash of the story? But as I continued along the Cerro Negro track to fetch our dogs, I mused over how my version of Rogelio's story was pretty typical of the way things were in rural Spain in the long, bad years after the Civil War. So I feel it may be worth sharing both versions with you, patient reader; and I hope it allows you some sense of the difficulties we anthropological ethnographers face.

CHAPTER 5

DEER LEAP

As Jesús and Bernardo had predicted, Chloé's last school year passed in a flash and, as she was often stopping over with friends in town, even my last attendance of the Bus Club came and went unheralded. But life was moving forward. Chloé had put her name down to study at Granada University, partly because this was where most of her *pandilla* were heading, but also, to our delight, because it was one of the few places in Spain where you can study both French and Chinese.

As Confucius himself might have reflected, there's no knowing how things will pan out. Ana and I had both travelled in China before Chloé was born and we were thrilled by the possibility of going back there to visit a daughter studying Mandarin. And given the virtual demise of the Spanish job market, we figured that this skill might give her some kind of leg-up. But before embarking on this, Chloé had another rite of passage to negotiate – her first proper job. This was to be a summer of working back in Britain with some friends of ours who make and sell ice cream.

And so it was, in the Welsh drizzle of early summer, that I pulled into Martin and Juliet's farm drive, near Abergavenny. For the next three months Chloé was going to travel with these friends around the music festivals of Britain, camping in fields and selling their indescribably delicious sheep's milk ice cream to overheated festival-goers. When they had suggested the job she had jumped at the chance – what teenager would pass up a summer of endless days of ice cream and live music and dance tents? I could tell, though, from her quietness on the journey down, that she was a little apprehensive: there was something just a touch subdued in her manner, or perhaps it was simply her English persona rising to surface above her Spanish, which tends more to the noisy and gregarious.

Nonetheless, Chloé was also clearly impatient for me to be on my way. This was her first job, her first move away from home, and she didn't need me crowding her pitch, arming her with advice and catching up with old friends. It was strange to reflect that my daughter had been edging along the branch for the last year or so and that now, with a minimum of flurry and flap, she was flying off into the wide world outside El Valero. As I drove back to London, I stared at the windscreen wipers as they first swept aside the massing droplets and then, with the inevitable downpour, shelved water from one side to the other, and a feeling of utter desolation settled over me. What on earth was going on? I had just been joking with friends and hugging my daughter goodbye, and all of a sudden I wanted to weep.

I tried to focus instead on Chloé's excitement at setting out into the world and beginning work, and as I did so the memories started to drift to the surface of a time over forty years ago when I too was making my first shaky start in the adult world of gainful employment.

It was not yet five, and still pitch-dark outside, as I sat in the brightly lit kitchen of my parents' house, waiting, mouth open and staring at the clock. The house was silent apart from the humming and gurgling of household appliances. The rest of the family were, very sensibly, still asleep. My mother's poodles lay in their respective baskets looking at me and wondering what was going on. I wondered what was going on, too. It was a new day dawning for me, my first day of work – if you don't count newspaper delivery.

My parents had beggared themselves sending me to an expensive school, with high hopes of some glittering future. Things were not looking good, though, from an academic point of view; I had never been that studious, and had scraped by without taking things too seriously. The best school report I had ever received, said: 'He has endeared himself to me by the subtlety with which he makes himself a nuisance.' Life was different back then: there didn't seem to be the urgency that there is now . . . and teachers had the time to be thoughtful and witty when writing disparaging reports.

A man called Denny Scott had landed me this first summer job. He lived in a bachelor flat around the corner from us, near Horsham, and devoted his leisure time to the tending of orchids. He was a most peculiar man, and drove an open-topped sports car in shirt sleeves all through the icy days of winter, only deigning to put the roof up as the heat of summer approached. At a cocktail party he had insinuated to my parents that he could get me a job as a builder's labourer for A.E. Farr of Westbury, Wilts, for whom he – rather unaccountably, as he seemed to have pots of money – worked as an occasional quantity surveyor.

This was a far cry from what my parents had intended for me, but from the effusiveness of their gratitude you'd have thought he had offered me a fast track through the Foreign Office. They were anxious at the time that I was about to fritter away the summer and blight my future with dreams of rock stardom, as a result of being the drummer of a school band. A few weeks of five and a half days of gut-busting labour for sixteen pounds cash in hand ought to drive such foolish notions from my adolescent brain. For my own part I was delighted: it was sixteen pounds more than anyone else was willing to give me, and, who could say, it might even cover the cost of buying my own drum kit. The band was called The Garden Wall, later Genesis.

'Brunt will pick you up at the bottom of the drive at half past five,' Mr Scott had informed me in his clipped patrician tones. 'Don't be late. I'm giving you a big chance here.'

As the hands of the clock moved towards five-fifteen, I slid off the kitchen stool, gathered my lunchbag and slipped quietly out of the house into the greying dark. An owl hooted, the gravel of the drive crunched loudly beneath my feet. I pulled my coat around me against the fresh damp air – it can be like that at the beginning of July – and savoured the silence of the morning. Not a light shone from the windows; a few dwindling stars and the first grey of the coming dawn lit my way. I felt a delicious and entirely novel sense of superiority over all those idle slobs who lingered still in the warmth of their respective beds, wrapped in unproductive slumber.

I stepped out onto the road wondering a little apprehensively what work would be like, conscious that this was a rite of passage, that I was moving at last from childhood into adulthood. I was excited, too, at the prospect of new experiences and people, new knowledge and skills. I was sixteen years old and bursting with dreams and hope.

At the end of the drive I could make out a car parked, its engine bubbling quietly. Inside, softly illuminated by the glow of a pipe, sat a short man with a hard hat on. I opened the passenger door and leaned in. 'Would you be Mister Brunt?'

The occupant slowly turned his head, considered

me for a moment, drew deep from his pipe, and in a rich Somerset burr said: 'I would. Jim Brunt's the name. Call me Jim. In you get; we don't want to be late now.'

'I'm Chris,' I said offering my hand to shake.

Jim looked for some time at the hand before shaking it, slowly and firmly. I climbed into the smoke-filled interior, and slowly, ever so slowly, Jim urged the old car out onto the empty road.

After a few minutes of painfully slow progress I felt the need to say something, to break the silence. I know it was only five thirty in the morning, but I had just walked briskly in the cold for fifteen minutes and was wide awake.

'Pleased to meet you, Jim,' I said breezily.

He seemed unaware that I had said anything. But after a considerable lapse of time, he removed one hand from the wheel, extracted the pipe from his mouth, and rather like a turtle, from beneath the carapace of the hard yellow hat, turned slowly towards me, considered my fatuous conversational gambit for a moment, and returned in silence to his earlier position.

For a while I contented myself with looking through the side windows, where the first light of the day was bringing a little colour to the fields and trees. Then I eased back in my seat and tried to doze. But no, it was all too exciting. I tried again: 'How far is it to the job . . . you know, the site?' I wasn't quite sure what to call it.

I looked over at Jim as he commenced the

process of replying. Out came the pipe, the head swivelled towards me, a moment's reflection.

'About forty-five minutes.'

I thought about this for a bit. 'So what time do we start work, then?'

A pained expression passed across his features. 'Eight.'

I considered this information and looked at my watch. It didn't seem to square up: in forty-five minutes it would be only half-past six. Why would a person want to get to work an hour and a half before it started? Obviously I didn't know much about the nature of work, but this didn't make any sense at all.

I decided to venture another question. 'Um, Jim?'

A withering look.

'Why are we getting there so early, then?'

Jim frowned and changed gear to negotiate a hill. He sucked deep on his pipe and shifted from one buttock to the other. It appeared that he hadn't heard. We kept silent for a while as we passed through Ockley and Beare Green, then turned off towards Abinger Hammer and Friday Street. The early morning light began to flood across the fields and woods, and the North Downs loomed before us.

Finally Jim had an answer, and he put in motion the mechanism to deliver it. 'I tell you what, Chris . . . I likes to get up an' breathe the fresh air 'fore any other bugger's 'ad a chance to fart in it.' And he permitted himself a little chuckle. I chuckled too, to show that I was not above enjoying such indelicacy, and for a few miles we chuckled on, both getting the most out of this sagacious little conceit.

At half-past six, give or take a minute or two, we pulled up in the middle of a beech wood. There was a brick bridge over a single-track railway and, in a small clearing by the road, a big green wooden hut. Jim fumbled with the keys of the hut and disappeared inside. I stood outside for a bit, breathing in that morning beechwood air as yet untainted by human flatulence, and then walked out on to the bridge and leaned on the low brick parapet. As I stood there the first rays of morning sunlight came shimmering and gleaming along the rails from Effingham Junction and Dorking.

During the journey I had managed, with some difficulty, to elicit from Jim the facts about the bridge. It was called Deer Leap Bridge and was a Victorian construction of dark brick and a certain architectural distinction. Unfortunately the weight limit was three and a half tons, and some lunatic lorry driver had seen fit to drive his fifteen-ton articulated lorry over it. This had cracked the bridge so badly that it was no longer deemed safe for traffic, and our job was to build a hideous and utterly undistinguished new concrete bridge beside the old one. The road, which was a little back lane winding through the woods, had been closed to traffic for months, so we had this idyllic spot entirely to ourselves.

Shivering a little and bored, I followed Jim into

the hut. He had made himself a cup of tea, which he was drinking from an enamel mug as he pored over yesterday's *Sun*. I sensed that he had no desire to chat, lost as he was in the paper. I sat down on the wooden bench and, in the absence of anything more edifying to read, leafed through an older copy of *The Sun* that lay to hand. Jim was engrossed in the sports pages. I have never been interested in sport, of any hue, and I didn't want Jim to catch me studying the topless models, which seemed to be just about the only other content of the paper, so I devoted my attention to what tiny sensational nuggets of news there were. After five minutes I could have repeated the lot by heart. I fidgeted for a bit and looked around the inside of the hut. In one corner were stacked the shovels, pickaxes and sledgehammers that I supposed would be the tools of my new trade. A gas ring provided the heat for the tea, and a big bucket on a box would have been intended, I supposed, for washing up. But it was still not even seven o'clock, so, to kill some time, I decided to go for a walk. I was sixteen years old, you will remember; there was time enough and more for killing, then.

Out on the bridge site I was confronted with the incomprehensible and arcane paraphernalia of civil engineering: the great bundles of steel rods, drums of unfamiliar oils, machines that smelt of stale diesel and mud, and a monster concrete mixer set amongst its mountainous landscape of sand and gravel. It was hard to make head or tail of it all, so I wandered up the road and into the woods. For half an hour I walked through the dripping woods, delighting in the dappled light on the great limbs of the trees, and all in a green sheen from the canopy of fresh summer leaves above. The beech hangers of the North Downs in Surrey have a special beauty all their own and, on this bright summer morning, it was all mine for the taking. I took it and went back to the hut.

Jim grunted and barely looked up from his paper. A car drew up outside, breaking the silence, and a minute later the door banged and a man burst in, stamping his boots on the wooden floor and sniffing loudly. He was a thin, powerfully built, middle-aged man with a crooked nose, tar-blackened stumps for teeth and a strand of black greasy hair hanging over his forehead. I rose to greet him, proffering my hand. 'How do you do?' I began.

He stopped dead; his jaw dropped; he considered me for a long, long moment in amazement and distaste. I looked at Jim in the hope that he might break this impasse by introducing us . . .

'Oo's the cunt, Jim?' said the man.

I just did not know how to react to a thing like this; it was so far from any of my previous experience. I wondered if I ought perhaps to hit him, but it didn't seem like a good idea at the time, so I didn't. I just stood rooted to the ground like, well . . . a cunt.

In a moment, more cars arrived, more banging of doors, the sound of shouted oaths, and with a thunderous stamping and laughing and coughing and farting, an unruly mob of big, dirty, foul-mouthed men in cement-spattered clothes crashed through the door. The hut was instantly filled with their enormous and oppressive presence as they lumbered and barged about in the narrow space between the tools and the tea table. I shrank a little into my corner. I was learning fast: I'd have been a fool to go for the formal introduction again.

There was big Frank, who drove the lorry; Terry, the toothless foreman carpenter, a past master of the filthy story; incomprehensibly Irish Mervyn, the digger driver; Jim Riley, a sinewy work-worn labourer, all bad temper and unpleasantness; and Scott, who drove the drott. Then there was Belgian Andy, in charge of the mixer, whose entire conversation revolved around sex; and a particularly fat and foul-mouthed slug of an individual whose name escapes me but who was a comic genius and in charge of the tea. And the man who had called me a cunt was Fred the crane driver, surprisingly likable and amusing. Then, just as everyone was settling themselves in for the start of the job, the door opened and a young man sidled in and unfurled his tattered flares from their bicycle clips. He was Dave the Student, who had dropped out of an engineering course at the local tech and was trying to save enough money for a trip to India. This then was the cast of characters who would fill my life for the next few months.

* * *

Jim Brunt was the foreman and thus it fell to him to keep this rabble of brutes under control, and get the broken bridge rebuilt. He was a gentle and amiable man, not a little bumbling, and, though the butt of constant ragging, most of the men seemed to hold him in respect and affection. He was the only one to wear a hard hat, which seemed to confer authority. Things were different then: you wore what you liked on site, no compulsory hard hats, steel-toed boots or hi-vis fluorescent vests. If there was any uniform, it was the blue donkey jacket which I too wore over my jeans and T-shirt and sneakers. I guess I was just lucky: during my time on the building site nothing unpleasant ever fell on my head, nothing penetrated my shoes, and I didn't get run down and crushed by a drott. I came through more or less unscathed.

The men slung their kit on hooks, gathered tools and lumbered out into the cool sunlit morning, each to fill his allotted task. Jim kept me back until everybody had left the hut. 'Right Chris, later on this mornin' there's a lorryload o' cement comin', but till then I want you bottomin' up behind Mervyn. Fetch yourself a shovel.'

This was the moment I had been waiting for: the work. Of course I hadn't a clue what 'bottoming up' might be, but I took a shovel and followed Jim outside. A surprising degree of order reigned, with the men each having embarked upon his allotted task. Mervyn's task was to dig a trench for some pipes with the JCB.

'I want you down in that 'ole wi' Jim Reilly there, an' bottom up, nice 'n' neat like. And mind the back actor now.'

I jumped down into the trench. There was not a lot of room down there, what with Jim Reilly, and Merv's back actor (the hydraulic arm on the back of a JCB). But Merv was good: they said he could pick up a sixpence with his back actor, or even scratch his balls. It was one thing keeping out of the way of the great mechanical arm; it was another keeping clear of the awful Jim Reilly. Reilly was around sixty, I should have guessed, and lacking in the merest shred of agreeableness; he would never offer anybody a friendly word nor a smile – he just wasn't made like that. What he did was work with a terrifying ferocity, jabbing and thrusting with pick or shovel, accompanying himself with a constant stream of the vilest invective.

'Bastards, I'll show the fuckers, this work's shit, shitty fuckin' shit . . . I'll rare up on 'em an beat the shit outa 'em . . . they're all bastards, every bloody man Jack of 'em!'

This unending and meaningless tirade of abuse was not aimed at anyone in particular, but it seemed to provide the energy that drove this horrible old man to ever greater feats of shovelling and pickaxing. As he worked, his elbows and arms flailed out in all directions and you had to take care not to catch a nasty blow from the pick or shovel, an occurrence that would have given Jim

73

Reilly immense satisfaction. To my surprise I heard mention that he had a missus and I found myself wondering what sort of a woman could live with such a man. It seemed unlikely that the marriage was a happy one, but love is a strange thing.

Bottoming up, it appeared, was a matter of finishing off neatly the job that Mervyn had done with his back actor, smoothing out the sides and taking off the little hillocks left by the machine. It was hard to get a look in, though, with Reilly there giving it all he had got. I managed a little poke here and there, but I would scarcely say that I had got the measure of bottoming up by the time Jim Brunt peered over the edge of the hole and told me to come on up and get the lorry unloaded.

A big flat-bed truck was waiting by the cement mixer, loaded with sacks of cement. Now, in the normal course of events there would always be a few people hanging around, not really involved in anything specific, and they could be called upon to help with whatever task presented itself; but whenever the cement lorry arrived everybody made themselves scarce, busied themselves with jobs that could under no circumstances be interrupted. Thus it fell to me, and to Dave the Student. 'The Student' was a pejorative term used with the utmost scorn by the men, and it soon came to apply to me, too.

Dave and I shook hands and grinned a grin of collusion and shared exclusion. 'It's the old story,' he said. 'Every bugger fucks off soon as the cement has to be unloaded.' Dave had been at Deer Leap for long enough to have absorbed something of the vernacular.

I looked uneasily at the mountain of cement bags on the lorry and quailed a little. This was an ordeal and a test – and I was very uncertain that I would be up to it.

'Don't worry, we'll just take it easy. Don't bust a gut.'

If anything was going to bust my gut it was going to be those cement bags. A cement bag weighed, then, one hundredweight, or fifty kilos, the weight of a small adult. You had to come up to the truck and brace yourself while the driver dropped a bag down from the top of the load onto your shoulder; then you would turn round and stagger twenty paces across uneven ground, and there bend and slip it off your shoulder onto a growing pile of cement bags.

At first, when that bag hit your shoulder, the tendency was to buckle at the knees, or the waist or the neck, or any other part of the body with a hinge. It was a colossal weight. And each bag was thickly coated with a layer of fine grey cement, which exploded all over you upon impact, filling your hair with fine grey powder as well as your eyes, your clothes and every pore of your body. The unthinkable weight of the sack ground the stuff into your shoulder, and there it burnt with ten thousand tiny lacerations.

It was hellish, utterly hellish, but I was young

and desperately keen to be able to do work, so, in the parlance of the building site, I rared up and tore into it, quickly developing the necessary strategies for coping. I blew a few; I dropped some, and I fell a couple of times, but little by little I began to master the art of carrying sacks of cement. I suppose it was all in the breathing and in the posture and handling the sack accurately, with just the right amount of weight before and just the right amount behind.

It went on and on and on. It was a ten-ton truck; there would have been about two hundred sacks on it and, with every other bugger making himself scarce, the whole lot went on the shoulders of Dave and me. When we had got it all off and stacked, shortly before lunchtime, I was teetering on my last legs, with a neck as raw and red as steak, and an indignant quivering in every muscle of my body. But I felt suffused with a simple pride: this was work, and I had done it. I hadn't bottled out.

Jim Brunt ambled over and looked dubiously at our pile of sacks. He lit a match and put it to his pipe.

'I want you bottomin' up some more, back down in that 'ole wi' Jim Reilly now, Chris.'

That evening Jim Brunt was, of course, the last to leave. I slept a deep and exhausted sleep as the old car ambled slowly down the lane through the woods. Back home I could barely eat for the pains in my body, and battled vainly for sleep through stiffness and cramps. Yet the whole experience had been exhilarating. Manual labour, I decided, was for me.

I rose again at four forty-five the next morning, prepared enough sandwiches to cram my lunch bag to bursting, chose a book, *Point Counter Point* by Aldous Huxley, for the long morning wait, and set off down the drive in the dark. As soon as I eased into the seat in Jim's car, I fell fast asleep and didn't wake up until we arrived at Deer Leap.

'We're pourin' today,' said Jim, unfolding *The Sun*. I wondered what pouring might be. Jim, lost in the paper, didn't seem inclined to expand upon the subject. He read while I slept again like a young animal.

'Get your shovel, Chris.'

I gathered up my shovel of the day before. Another tiny frisson of pleasure, my own shovel, and it was a beast of a shovel too: not some half-arsed gardening tool, but a proper Eastman, the type used by the navvies who built the first railways. A man's tool . . . and when you're sixteen this means something. I staggered out of the hut; my bones and muscles still hurt like hell from the cement bags.

I was to work on the mixer where Belgian Andy was clattering about in readiness for the pouring.

'D'yo 'ave it in las' nite?' he shouted down at me.

'I beg your pardon,' I shouted back. Andy's

accented English was all but impossible to understand. He made an unspeakably lewd gesture.

Dave, who was leaning on his shovel at the foot of a hill of gravel, translated for my benefit. There were shouts and the rumbling of machinery; the pouring was ready to start. 'Just shovel,' said Dave. 'Shovel till you can shovel no more.' And we bent our backs to those big old Eastman shovels.

Beside the mixer was a huge double pair of scales. Our job was to shovel sand into one half of it, until we got to 850 kilos, then spin it round and fill the other half with 1,600 kilos of gravel. When it was full the scales would tip into the mixer, where Andy would add the cement. Once the hopper was empty, we started shovelling again.

We started with the sand; sand was easy because you can get a huge load on the shovel and if you're placed right it's just a deep satisfying thrust into the pile, a twist of the body, a superhuman heave of the arms and that's twenty kilos down. The gravel was different: you can only get so much on the shovel, much of it falls off, and it's hard to drive the shovel into the pile. On pouring days Dave and I were the motive power of the whole site. Everybody depended on us for the great loads of concrete to be shifted, poured into the shuttering, and vibrated, and so whenever we flagged, we would be lashed with the most hideous abuse from all sides. In the main this would be good-natured chaffing, but if we got too far behind, tempers would sometimes flare.

We worked, even on cold days, stripped to the waist, warmed by the sunshine and the herculean labour, which tore at the skin of our hands, leaving fearful blisters which immediately burst and filled with grit and cement and started suppurating. Nobody would think of wearing gloves, though; it wouldn't have gone down well, wouldn't have been manly . . . and, for better or for worse, manly was what it was all about.

One day, there was an accident. Scott was using his drott to haul out a colossal ten-ton trunk of oak. A drott is a tiny open bulldozer, all engine and a huge powerful toothed grab for a shovel. Anyway, Scott was heaving this tree backwards but it was heavier than the drott, so as he raised the shovel, instead of raising the load, it raised the drott itself in the air, so that it was tiptoeing backwards on the tips of its caterpillar tracks. This seemed to work alright, though, so Scott kept on coming. Then suddenly the drott hit a bump and slammed back down on the ground, whereupon the colossal oak tree rolled down the arms of the shovel and right over Scott. He screamed and managed to duck beneath the bonnet just enough to save himself from having the life crushed out of him. He was badly hurt, and was rushed out in an ambulance to hospital.

Later in the mess hut there was a silence as everybody thought over the awful thing that had happened.

'Poor Scottie,' somebody said. 'Fuckin' awful thing to 'appen to a bloke.'

Some heads were nodded, then a brief silence, until Frank said, echoing everybody's unspoken view, 'Yeah, but 'e didn't oughter of screamed.'

'Nah,' everyone agreed.

'That's right,' concurred Terry. 'It wasn't manly.'

I wondered if my own nascent manhood would stand the test of a ten-ton tree trunk rolling towards me, without uttering a sound. I knew now that you were not supposed to scream, but it wouldn't be easy.

The pouring went on all day long; there were hundreds of tons of concrete to fill each lift. For Dave and me it was the most mind-numbing repetitive work hour after hour, with barely a break, but you didn't need to think much, so we amused ourselves by telling stories and jokes and horsing about. The pain in our hands and the pull on our muscles were fearful, but if you're young and well fed your body puts on muscle very quickly and after a couple of weeks I was hard and tight as a drott.

We poured every third day. On the other days Dave and I had it a little easier, down in the hole bottoming up with the vile Jim Reilly, or helping out with the shuttering and steel-tying. The day after the concrete was poured, we would break out the shuttering, the plywood mould that gave the poured concrete the desired form, according to the plans for the bridge. Then we would spend a day and a half perched precariously above the railway lines, constructing the steel skeleton that would form the next lift of the pier of the bridge.

This was a complex web of steel reinforcing rods that we would tie together, armed with pliers, tape measure and a roll of tying wire. And then finally we oiled the shuttering boards with fish oil, so that they could be broken out easily for the next lift, and lashed, nailed and bolted them into place, ready to hold the hundred tons or so of sloppy concrete from the next pour.

I cannot remember ever feeling so vital and alive. I was a teenager, of course, and that had a lot to do with it, but there was something about the fiercely hard physical work out in the open air. It felt good to be tanned and muscular and powerful and dirty, and always, seemingly, teetering on the verge of laughter.

The men were raunchy and funny, utterly unselfconscious, and always ready with a scurrilous story or joke. Money was tight: their cars were wrecks, not one of them owned his house, but they were neither wretched nor miserable. I loved being with them, and was happy as a hen when they accepted me – almost – as one of them.

One morning, the foreman carpenter came into the mess hut rather the worse for wear. He sat down with his mug of tea at the wooden table and said, rather enigmatically, 'I pissed on me own teeth las' nite.'

The assembled company looked up quizzically from their mugs and crumpled copies of *The Sun*. Terry burped loudly to make sure he had everyone's full attention.

'We was down the Angel an' I'd 'ad a dozen beers or so, too much really, so I ducks out to the toilets to barf it all up. I leans over and shoots the lot into the gutter, but fucked if I don't shoot me teeth out with it. Just that moment a load of blokes comes in, they was well gone, and one of 'em says, "'Ere look, some fucker's lost 'is teeth; let's piss on 'em!" I wasn't going to let on they was mine, was I?, so I keeps me mouf shut an' joins in wiv 'em, an' there I was grinnin' away an' pissin' on me own teeth as they floats past. I 'ad to go back in there later on an' fish 'em out.'

'Scrubbed up nice, though, ain't they?' he concluded, flashing us a pearly grin.

Terry was a natural storyteller, and by the time he finished telling this appalling tale the whole hut was heaving with laughter.

And so the long days of summer passed and the hideous concrete bridge grew, and I learned how to hold my own in the exchange of obscenities that passed for bonhomie among my workmates. And I learned how to work, to give my strength and skill – or, rather, sell it, as I was earning sixteen pounds a week for this – for some cooperative endeavour. I learned, too, how to use a pick and a shovel and a sledgehammer, and it was learning that has stood me in good stead all my life.

Chloé had just finished her first month on the festival circuit when Martin of Shepherds' Ice Cream phoned. They had been unlucky with the weather: the rain had been torrential and ceaseless; the tents had been waterlogged; the vans had got bogged, and some of the bands had cancelled. 'But Chloé was great,' he told us. Apparently she had dealt with everything – the mud, the weariness, the occasional crazy customer – with good-natured efficiency and tact and, even after an all-night party, had turned up looking fresh as a daisy in the morning, acting as if her life's sole ambition was to sell more ice cream. 'She's a terrific worker,' Martin went on. 'You should be proud. I'd have her back any year.'

I was. To discover that your offspring has what it takes to earn an honest wage is a pleasing discovery indeed.

CHAPTER 6

A 4B PENCIL

I have never been much of a one for competition. My grandfather would try and instil some sense of the competitive spirit in me by looking at me earnestly (his name was actually Ernest, though he loathed and never used it) and saying, 'Remember, Christopher: the race is always to the swift.' But even as a nipper I thought this a peculiarly daft and unedifying piece of nonsense.

First of all, life is not a race, or, if it was, then it would be more like Alice's Caucus race, that great sporting event in Wonderland, where, at a given signal, all the competitors would start milling aimlessly about and, upon another signal, would stop where they were. Alice, if I remember rightly, was incensed at the futility of this, but to me a Caucus-race seems just the ticket. Instead of busting a gut in order to be first, it may be better just to mill about and enjoy the view and the pleasure of encounters with others. And if there's a race to be run at all, then I'd much prefer to be jogging along at the back, with the idlers, the dreamers, the wanderers and philosophers.

Yet there are times when we have no option but to gird our loins and join the fray, jostling shoulders with the pack hurtling swiftly along. And without exception these outbreaks of competitive zeal are spurred by, and entered on behalf of, our offspring. In this case the impetus was provided by the need to register Chloé for her university place. By some quirk of planning the enrolment for the Chinese part of the course was on a different day to the others, and it was a day on which Chloé happened to be in some muddy field of England selling ice cream. So at six o'clock on a July morning we sprang from the bed in order to get to the city in good time.

El Palacio de las Columnas on Puentezuelas is where the Faculty of Translation and Interpretation at Granada University holds court, and at ten to eight Ana and I were standing outside the great door with its serpentine marble columns. We felt the tiniest bit intimidated, perhaps because neither of us had made it to university, but more because we knew with ghastly certainty that we would have failed in some infinitesimal particular of document-gathering and form-filling required by the faculty, and we would be upbraided by the administrative staff and made to feel the fools we feared we were.

Registration did not start until nine, but even so we were not the first there. We sidled up and introduced ourselves to the smart blonde woman and her daughter, who had beaten us to first place

in the queue. She was English, for heaven's sake
. . . it was to be a good half-hour before the first
Spaniard turned up. We felt a little sheepish, being
so early, and also being English. . . but we had
somehow got wind of the fact that registration for
the Chinese department was on a first come, first
served basis, and there were only fifty places, a
fact that not many others seemed to know.

Ana is good at administrative stuff and had
gathered all the required documentation and put
it in a big file, which she was leafing through now,
and asking me questions to which I did not know
the answers. I was along for the bulk and body
mass, in case it came to a scrimmage over who
was attended to first.

Soon the first Spaniards began to turn up and
an amorphous melee began to surge up the steps
and around the door. We kept tight to our preeminent spot. 'Stick close to me and be ready to do
as you're told,' ordered my wife.

Under normal circumstances queuing is a most
orderly business in Spain, although it may not
appear so to the uninitiated. It's like this: you enter
the place where you're going to do your queuing,
look around and ask, somewhat bafflingly, '*¿Quien
hace las veces?*' ('Who makes the times?'), whereupon the last person in the queue will turn to you,
and say, 'It's me.' So now all you have to do is
keep an eye on one person; you can amble over
to talk to a friend, find somewhere to sit, or even
wander off for a bit, once you've made the time

yourself. When the person who has 'made the times' for you makes a move, then you're on next. This system works very well, but it doesn't look good; it hasn't the neatness of a good orderly line. And of course the whole shebang breaks down when there are foreigners involved who don't know the score.

But on the steps of the Palacio de las Columnas that morning, as the first hot rays of sunshine came pouring over the house tops and down into the street, the orderly queuing system was nowhere to be seen. The place was full of parents, all of them having clearly been laid on the line by their kids, and these parents were in pugnacious mode, ready to fight like rats for the furtherance of their children's future.

On the dot of nine the door opened and we were washed in on the head of the flood. Somehow we managed to present our documentation amongst the first half-dozen petitioners, but then we were all given new forms and told to come back when we had done so. They had to be filled in – and there were the direst of consequences for not complying with this order – with a 4B pencil.

We ratched about in our bags, but neither of us had anything resembling a 4B pencil; I don't think anybody did – after all, you don't generally carry a 4B with you, do you? The flood of parents headed in dribs and drabs back out onto the street in search of the all-important utensil. We went to a bar in

Plaza Trinidad and, while Ana ordered herself a coffee and started getting to grips with the new form, I was despatched to find a pencil.

This proved more taxing than one would have imagined, as there wasn't a stationers to be seen for miles around. I wandered hither and thither, ducking fruitlessly in and out of shops that I thought with a little imagination might conceivably sell 4Bs . . . but no luck. Perhaps some rat had received advance information about the pencils, and had bought up all the stock within a three-kilometre radius of the faculty, and was even now, unctuous and alone, handing over the correctly filled-in form. People will sink pretty low.

And then a cry, 'Cristóbal! What are you doing here?' I spun round. It was none other than Pinhole Johnny, so called because of his consummate artistry with the pinhole camera.

'Hey, Johnny. Good to see you.' I was really pleased to have bumped into him, hadn't seen him for ages. There was a lot to talk about.

'Shall we go for a coffee?' he said.

'Er . . . I can't really, right now. I'm on a serious mission. You don't happen to have a 4B pencil on you, do you?'

He fumbled about in his bag. 'Nope, no such luck. I've got an HB, oh, and a 2B even . . . will that do? Or how about two 2Bs stuck together?'

'This is no time for facetiousness, Johnny. It's got to be a 4B.'

'I tell you what, there's a printer around the corner; they do a lot of work for me and they're bound to have one. Let's go and see them.'

So we went round to the printers and after a little negotiation they promised to lend Johnny their 4B pencil so long as he promised to bring it back. It appeared that the 4B was as scarce as hens' teeth in this part of the city.

By the time I got back to the bar with Johnny, Ana was in a state of some agitation. I think she felt that I was not taking the business seriously enough and had been off somewhere fooling around with Pinhole Johnny, as opposed to wearing the soles of my shoes to the bone in the search for that 4B pencil.

Ana set to filling in the form while I ordered a couple more coffees. 'Do you think we count as minors?' she asked, her brow furrowed with wondering.

This stumped me. It seemed an odd question: if you were still a minor at fifty-something, then who *wasn't* one?

'No, miners,' she elucidated. 'It seems there are certain advantages to be had if you're employed down a mine.'

'Who has to be the miner, Chloé or us?'

'The parents, I should think, although it's far from clear.'

'Probably not, then. I think that might be swinging the lead a bit.' And with that the form was filled in to the best of our ability and Johnny was sent back to the printers with the pencil, while we went back to the Palacio de las Columnas.

The 4B pencil ruse had thinned out the crowd of parents, but you still had to claw and thump your way through just to be seen. At last, though, we were in sight of the final desk, behind which sat the bespectacled dragon of a woman who would have the final word over Chloé's destiny. We stood before her, a respectable distance from the desk, and dithered a little, timidly proffering the 4B form, when suddenly a balding short-arsed man shot in front of us and sat himself down at the chair before the desk, spreading his documentation like a card sharp. I gaped like a dying cod, seeking the words of righteous indignation, but it was too late: the bastard, still panting slightly – he had clearly just shouldered his way through from the street – had launched into a carefully prepared peroration and was already in full flight, a full flight that we, with our inept country Spanish, would never be able to match. Why, I believe the dragon woman had already sized us up and was thinking, Oho, here's a couple of half-witted foreigners and they won't understand anything and they'll have filled out the form all wrong, and they'll barely speak Spanish. Heaven help us.

She shot us a glance as the baldy rabbited ingratiatingly on. 'I think you'll find everything in order here, señora – I've filled out the form myself – I had to do it because my son is in Canada right now having won a scholarship to a prestigious language school in Montreal – he is a terrific linguist you see, speaks four languages, amongst them Hungarian, does it in his spare time for his own amusement – I know he'll be a great credit to the . . .'

The woman administrator peered at him owlishly as he delivered this torrent of codswallop, and then lowered her eyes to his impeccable form. She scanned it, then looked up at him and raised a finger. 'Everything seems to be in order here, señor.' She paused. 'Except that it appears you have used an HB pencil for the form. I'm afraid our computer will not accept that. You'll have to go over the little boxes with a 4B pencil, then come back and present the form once more.' She gave him the most charming of smiles and handed back the form, then smiled at us and beckoned us to sit down.

There used to be a bar in the university building, ostensibly for the students, but it was such a hell of a good bar that everybody in the neighbourhood soon got wind of it and packed the place out, and the poor students, who had the disadvantage of having from time to time to attend lectures, found themselves unable to get within even shouting distance of the bar . . . so they closed it down. This was a shame, as we would dearly have liked to buy that dragon woman a drink, especially when she said to us that we had made a terrific job of filling in the form and that Chloé was to present herself at the Faculty to commence her studies at the beginning of September.

CHAPTER 7

VIRTUAL CHICKENS

Few excitements in life can compare with finding a new-laid egg nestling in the bright golden straw of a corner of the hen house. I've yet to meet a child unmoved by such a discovery, and even for adults, like myself, it's pretty good. I would argue that the contemplation of the aesthetic beauty of an egg – the very acme of perfection and, if you happen to be an alligator, a turtle or a chicken, the cradle of existence – transports us to thoughts of the sublime.

The finest way we can express this is by elaborately preparing them for our consumption. And of all the wonderful ways there are, you can do no better than fry them. An egg fried in hot, deep spitting olive oil with the brown, crispy bits around the edges and the rich deep-yellow yolk still liquid but with just a hint of viscosity and barely covered with a pale film of heated albumen . . . well, this is about as near an approximation of felicity as you can get. Scrambled eggs come hot on the heels of the fried ones, and it's a marvellous way to get rid of a glut of eggs. Two of you ought to be able to deal with five of them. Make perfect golden toast and put it on a plate. If you live north roughly of the 45th parallel, then you'll want some butter on the toast; anywhere south of that and you're better off with olive oil. Break four of the eggs in a bowl and just the yolk of the fifth; this makes it a bit yellower. Beat 'em up a bit and tip into a pan in which you have heated some butter and oil. Cook slowly and don't stop stirring with a wooden spoon even for a minute. Take the pan off the heat while the eggs are still shiny and runny; they'll keep on cooking. Tip the mix onto the toast and shave with a potato peeler some smoked cod's roe on top, a hint of tabasco and a big pinch of pepper and maybe a peck of parsley.

Now what you need for eggs is, of course, chickens. Unfortunately at El Valero we had lost the chickens when the chicken-run wall collapsed and the fox got in and wolfed – in a manner of speaking – the lot. Ana and I were desolate, and we felt the impact of this loss all the more acutely when Chloé left home at the start of the university term to move into a flat in Granada. If getting Chloé up and out to catch the school bus was the great imperative that got us rolling in the morning, then feeding the chooks ran it a close second and for a time we lived a rudderless existence.

Added to this, we had no reason now to save the scraps of food that we used to put aside so assiduously, knowing that they were not mere leftovers but tasty ingredients of a future meal. It takes a lot of the fun and dash out of cooking when you know there's no margin left for error; no chickens to polish off the unpalatable bits, the failed experiments or the portions excess to requirements that remain in the bottom of the pan. It offended our frugal country habits and natural inclination towards recycling, but most of all it pained us that we had no eggs to send to Chloé, who, having shown little interest in farm produce while living at home, had developed a passion for home-grown fruit and vegetables as soon as she moved away. She was on a mission, she told us, to buck up her flatmates' ideas about healthy eating and impress upon them the sound economy of relying on nature's own larder rather than waste good partying money on the ready-made muck sold at the local *supermercado*.

To return to our chicken-led way of life, I needed to repair their run, and this time it would have to be the sort of run that would last them, and us, for the rest of our days. Time was marching on and the last thing I wanted to be doing in ten years' time was to start all over again on the poultry. A good solid chicken run ought to take the place of the pensions and insurances that we have always seen fit to avoid.

So I built the chicken run and I built it well, adopting a nice compromise between art and fortification. The next step was to people it with chickens. Quite by chance, Ana had come across a superlative poultry website on the Internet and jotted down the address. We booted up her horrible old computer, a thing with no R nor P nor apostrophe on it, and launched ourselves into the World Wide Web. There was the webpage and they had every sort of chicken and fowl you could dream of. There were photos of them and descriptions of their qualities and advantages, and, lo and behold, in some cases, they even had them starring in their own videos. We could audition our chickens online.

First of all we decided to check out the Andalusian Blue. It was represented in a five-minute video clip. We clicked the right arrow and waited with excitement for the film to upload. Ah yes, there it was, a real stonker of a chicken. It was standing on some beaten earth near a cornfield. We watched as it stared in a desultory manner at the camera and then turned its head to look to the left for a while. Then, getting bored with that, it looked to the right. There was an atmospheric soundtrack that consisted of some water dripping and crickets doing their stuff. After a while the chicken decided to look straight ahead again, giving us an excellent view of its beak.

I looked at Ana, then back at the screen. The chicken was still looking straight ahead. Ana then looked at me. I was looking at the screen. I was still enjoying the video, although I had to admit that it was a bit short on action. You sort of felt that something was going to come along and grab the chicken, a scenario with which we were only too horribly familiar, but one which you couldn't help feel would add something to the plot. Nothing came along to grab the chicken, though. It shifted its weight and looked down at the ground, a bit bashfully, I thought.

'Christ, it's like watching an Ingmar Bergman film,' I said.

'Ssh,' Ana admonished. 'I think something's happening.'

The chicken looked up again and twitched. There were a few wisps of dried grass on the ground. I believe the chicken was thinking about pecking them. Occasionally they shifted a little as some infinitesimal zephyr passed. The chicken looked down at them again. I looked at Ana again. I like Ana; I've lived with her for a long time. It was a hot evening and she was wearing one of those strappy little tops. I was starting to get bored with the film and just a little amorous. I slipped my arm round her shoulders. She turned and frowned at me.

'Look,' she said. 'We're supposed to be choosing chickens. What do you think of the Andalusian Blue?'

'It's OK,' I said, noncommittally.

And so on to the Lords. These were the ones with bald necks like vultures, hideous to look at but a beast in the egg-laying department. We reckoned them marginally more interesting on screen than the Andalusian Blues; they seemed to have more charisma. At long last the credits began to roll on the Lords, too. Five minutes can be a long time. But whatever the longueurs of the videos, any chicken fancier worth their salt had to admit that the selection was truly impressive. Things had come a long way since a poultry van from Ciudad Real would come to Órgiva every Friday, stacked to the gunwales with partridges, quails, guinea fowl and chickens.

We chose a couple of the Andalusian Blues, a couple of Lords, a couple of Prats (don't ask me why), and a grey cock. After we pressed the appropriate keys, delivery would be by courier within twenty-four hours. We set about putting the final touches to the chicken run.

Amazingly, the very next afternoon the chickens arrived in town. They came packed in two custom-made cardboard boxes in a little van. I drove them home and Ana and I gathered in the chicken run, having made a very heaven of it, to release them. As always with poultry, they lurked in the corner looking unutterably depressed. Ana suffers deep anguish about this, but I am more sanguine, and do not attribute to the humble hen either the limitless subtlety or the broad range of emotions that we higher beings enjoy. Poultry are either depressed or alright; there are no middling shades of grey. And I imagine that the experience of being grabbed and stuffed into a cardboard box and then shipped for four hours would tend towards the depressing rather than the uplifting. Until something positive occurred to convince them otherwise, they would remain depressed.

So we went down to the farm in search of the

sort of positive thing that we thought would make a chicken feel alright. It would have to be food because, along with sex, food is the only thing chickens are interested in, and these were too young to care much about sex, which was perhaps just as well, because the sort of sex that chickens have looks pretty ghastly, particularly for the poor hen.

So we got them some *Robinia pseudoacacia* leaves, alfalfa, dandelions, vervain and chickweed. Fortunately the vegetable garden is always rich in greenery, and Ana knows exactly what chickens love and what they don't like at all. Funny that they should love the *Robinia*, the black locust tree, because in order to check the spelling I looked it up on the Web, only to find that the leaves contain robin, a toxin that gives horses anorexia, depression, incontinence, colic, weakness and cardiac arrhythmia. It's probably a question of dose.

We lovingly arranged bunches of all these plants around the place, but the young chickens only looked at them with deepest suspicion . . . and now I know about the *Robinia* I'm not surprised. We tried them with oranges, apricots, plums and loquats, all the most delicious fruits in season, but even this failed to raise their enthusiasm.

By now we had reinstated our old 'chicken bucket' to its pride of place on the kitchen counter and once more began to throw in all the leftovers that we believe chickens like: lettuce and carrots, cucumbers and parsley. These have to be chopped up into peck-sized pieces. Potato peelings have to be boiled a bit, but then they like them, along with rice and pasta. The detritus of prawns is popular with most chickens, too . . . but what really gets them going is, I'm afraid to say, chicken. It is by a long head their favourite thing. Urban friends and visitors are appalled to see us giving chicken scraps to the chickens, but only because they don't know the score, the way things are in the country.

Chicken and prawns are not something we eat that often, so the air of depression continued for some weeks, with the whole lot of them huddled miserably in a corner of the chicken run, until Ana went in to feed and water them, whereupon they would scatter in a terrified squawking panic. There was no sign of any eggs; they were too young for that. Soon the depression started to get to Ana.

'I wonder about these chickens,' she said. 'They're no fun at all and they don't lay any eggs.'

'Be patient, dear,' I suggested. 'All in its own sweet time.'

As the weeks went by the chickens began to get big and beautiful; the lavish feeding routine was paying off. And then one day Ana returned ecstatically from the chicken run holding the first egg. After that the eggs came in veritable cascades; we were getting five a day and often a big double-yolker, for which, according to the chicken website, the Prats were famous. A sense of gladness pervaded our lives as the larder began to fill.

Before long we had reached that interesting state where production was beginning to exceed demand.

It occurred to us that, just as we had needed the chickens to relieve us from the burden and waste of left-over food, we now needed Chloé back to relieve us from the glut. Neighbours were no help as they all had chickens themselves, and, although we could have fed the eggs to the dogs, it seemed excessive and a waste, because dogs don't appreciate the qualities of a good egg. The occasional egg-and-home-produce run to Chloé's Granada lodgings seemed like the best solution, and a fine, unobtrusive way to keep in touch.

CHAPTER 8

BREAKFAST IN MEDINA SIDONIA

The phone – it was Michael. Michael being my good friend and travel companion Dr Michael Jacobs, art historian, author, stuttering raconteur and formidable cook, calling from his home in Frailes, a village not far to the north of us, near Jaén.

'Ah, Chris . . . erm . . . I've got myself into a b-bit of a scrape. You see, Cuqui has asked me to be president of the jury at a *concurso gastronómico* in C-Conil. It's tuna, the *almadraba* – the spring tuna harvest.'

'Mmm,' I said. 'Tuna is by a long head my favourite fish, although . . .'

'Mine, too. But I can't possibly do it.'

'You what?'

'I can't possibly do it,' he said again, with an unusual air of finality.

'Why ever not?' I expostulated. 'You must be bonkers. It'll be the best tuna you've ever eaten.'

'Yes, but . . . well . . . I'm trying to get this wretched b-book written and so saying no to absolutely everything, and as you know I don't drive, and going all the way to Conil on public transport will take me the best part of a week there and back. It's out of the question. I'm not doing it.'

I could tell what was coming next; sure enough it came:

'Y-you don't want to d-do it, do you?'

'Come on, Michael. I couldn't possibly be president of the jury at a *concurso gastronómico* . . .'

'Of course you could; all you have to do is eat the tuna – admittedly rather a lot of tuna – and then say nice things about it. It's easy as that. You could d-do it in your sleep.'

'I really can't, Michael. I'm trying to get a book finished too, and I've got the *acequia* to clean and the sheep to shear . . . I'm right up against it. I mean, it sounds very tempting but I really can't. I'm sorry.'

And so we said no more about it. And then I thought about it a bit and, as it got nearer supper time and as I began to feel a little bit peckish, the idea of that tuna began to seem more and more tempting. Also I was looking for material for an article or two, and it seemed likely that on a jaunt of this nature something worthy of an article or two would be bound to happen. Neither should one forget the old adage that 'All work and no play makes Jack a dull boy.'

So I rang Michael and told him that I would do it.

'That's marvellous, Chris. I'll ring Cuqui right away; she'll be delighted.'

Next there was a silence while a thought occurred to him . . .

'You know what?' he continued. 'I've been thinking and I th-thought that if you're going to go along, then p-perhaps I might c-come along too, and you could pick me up?'

'Well, that would be lovely, Michael,' I lied (for I had rather wanted to be the president of a jury, the first and probably the last time in my life that I would be president of anything). 'But surely we can't both be the president . . . can we?'

Another silence, a short one. 'You can be the p-president,' he said, magnanimously.

'Oh, I couldn't possibly,' I, with false modesty, replied.

There was yet another pause while Michael pondered how best to put something.

'Actually, I wasn't telling the whole truth about the p-president. Neither of us will be p-president; in fact, there isn't a president.'

'But surely there has to be a president; you can't have a jury without a president.'

'Er . . . these sort of juries d-don't actually have presidents. They don't work like that. They're different.'

'Then why,' I rounded on him, 'did you say you were going to be president?'

'S-sometimes one says things to make things seem a b-bit more interesting than they really are. This was one of those. There is no president.'

★   ★   ★

106

Michael was right about Conil being a long way away. I looked on the Internet and it seemed that by an unimaginably convoluted route it would be four hours and twenty-two minutes from Granada . . . and Granada is an hour and a half from home! Six hours driving west in the evening, squinting into the lowering sun, hunched over a wheel. I would barely be able to walk by the time we got there.

Still, the sky was a hazy blue and the northern slopes of the Sierra Nevada were white with thick snow that shone in the afternoon sunlight as I pulled into the bus station of Granada to pick up my friend.

'Ay, Andalucía,' he exclaimed. 'What a paradise!' And it was: out towards Santa Fe the River Genil was rushing full and clear amongst the great groves of whispering poplars that seem like armies laying siege to the city from the west. As we raced along towards Loja and Antequera the land began to roll with hills of asparagus and corn, still green and shot with scarlet seams of poppies.

'Ooh,' said Michael.

'Aah,' I concurred.

A little later, as we spun past the lorries lumbering up the Cuesta Blanca near Salinas, we each gasped anew at the great pinnacles of bare rock that burst from the fertile earth of the valleys of the Montes de Málaga.

'D'you know what that one's called?' asked Michael, indicating an extravagantly shaped colossus of rock soaring to the south of the motorway. I didn't, or I'd forgotten; one or the other. 'It's El Peñón de los Enamorados – Lovers' Cliff – and of course there's a cock-and-bull story that goes with it, the usual thing of a Moorish princess and a Christian prince whose love was impossible and so they threw themselves in the time-honoured fashion off the cliff and were dashed together on the rocks below. And, predictably enough, in the popular imagination the shape of the rock is that of the princess, lying down, or her h-head, at any rate.'

We pondered this singular phenomenon together. 'Can't you see it?' said Michael.

I couldn't. The rock resembled nothing so much as an amorphous lump of rock. But as we zoomed past, it did indeed begin to change shape . . . and suddenly I saw it. 'She has a hooked nose like a beak, and a receding forehead, like a Cro-Magnon hag on a bad day. It seems unlikely your Christian prince would fall for a girl who looked like that.'

'Ah yes, but you've missed it. A minute ago, while you were overtaking those lorries, she was perfection itself – the ideal f-feminine physiognomy.'

For a while we wondered at the transience of beauty, but at our age it wasn't a subject that we particularly wished to dwell upon.

'Th-there's a slight p-problem with the judging of the tuna competition,' began Michael.

I began to smell a rat. I knew there would be a rat; there always is.

'Go on.'

'Well, you know there are two c-categories: the innovative and the tr-traditional.'

'Yes, you said that. I want to judge the innovative category, and seeing as how I'm not going to be president, then I think I ought to be granted that little whim. I like raw tuna best and I think that it'll be less likely to have had the living daylights boiled out of it in the innovatory line, no?'

'Y-yes, b-but you can't,' said Michael, a little defensively, I thought.

'Why ever not?'

'B-because I shall be j-judging the innovators and you'll b-be with the traditionals.'

This seemed manifestly unjust, but I waited for an explanation.

'You see, C-Cuqui is submitting a dish in the traditional and I've known Cuqui for a long long time and so I will feel it inc-cumbent on me to make sure she wins . . . out of f-friendship you understand. And so because everybody knows that I know Cuqui – and I've known Cuqui for thirty years – I'm not allowed to judge the category she's in. It's b-bad enough my even b-being here, but then it was Cuqui herself who g-got me the g-gig.'

'Gig' is not a word that Michael uses that much.

We had left the *autovía* now and were zooming along a long straight road between fields of garlic and cotton on the way to Campillos. Michael, as always on such occasions, was watching me with admiration and bewilderment as, nonchalantly and almost unconsciously, I controlled the headlong flight of the great steel beast in which we were so comfortably cocooned. Michael has never learned to drive. To impress him I casually switched on the windscreen wipers and sprayed the screen, ostensibly to clear the thick film of insects that had seen fit to immolate themselves against our hurtling juggernaut. It was easy, just an almost imperceptible flick of a finger. 'I may not know much about art history,' I enthused, 'but after all these years I sure know how to drive a car.'

The further west we travelled the more the beautiful blue *Echium* took over from the poppies. We oohed and aahed all the more as we wound among whole hillsides of deep blue. Michael, out of academic interest, was plotting our course on his accursèd iPhone, which was unnecessary as a) I knew the way, b) I had a printed route description off the internet, and c) it was signposted.

'We'll be in Olvera before long,' he said, fingering the wretched device.

'I know; I'm looking at it, on that hill up ahead.'

In a similar vein, without actually looking at it, Michael announced our imminent arrival at Medina Sidonia.

'I think it's my favourite town in all of Spain,' he continued. 'It's exquisitely beautiful, and there's a bar that's the most perfect bar and it does the perfect breakfast.'

'Well, I've never been there, so perhaps we can

have breakfast there on the way home on Wednesday morning.' This, I figured, would be a useful gambit to get Michael on the move early so that we could each arrive home in time to put in a respectable showing on the respective books we were supposedly writing.

'Yes, that would be good; we can get an early morning hit of pig fat.'

The mere mention of the pig fat made us both think how hungry we were. It was getting on for that time of day. The last rays of the sun were setting over the sea as we pulled into Conil. I staggered from the car, shook myself and delved in the back for my needments: the beloved Marrakech Medina leather man-bag containing on this occasion the single necessary item for spending the night in places other than my own dear bed – that is, an ageing blue toothbrush. I also had with me a rather disgusting Panama hat with a brown sweat stain oozing from the hatband at the front, and a cherished pale corduroy jacket, part of the only suit I have ever owned. I bought it over thirty-five years ago and, although it costs me dear to squeeze the lower half of my person into the trouser, the jacket still fits – so long as I hold my breath and stand up straight – like the proverbial glove.

Michael emerged from behind the car. To my surprise and delight, he was dressed almost identically: Panama hat, beige jacket, black jeans and leather man-bag. He stopped and looked at me in consternation.

'God,' he said. 'We look like a couple of old, gay ice-cream salesmen.'

I had to admit that he was right. I bristled a little, though, at the slight to my jacket. 'This jacket, I'll have you know, Michael, is proper class,' and I held it open so that he could admire the prestigious if rather frayed label on the inside pocket. 'It dates from the days when things were made well; I've had it for over thirty-five years . . .'

'It certainly looks like it,' he observed.

Following the directions suggested by Michael's telephone, we entered the labyrinth of the town, looking for the hotel that the Tourist Board had booked us into. I had been to Conil once before, with Ana on the way to Cádiz, if I remember rightly. It was round about lunchtime and the Wife's blood sugar levels were hitting the floor, so we stopped and installed ourselves at a restaurant on the front. We decided, for some reason which escapes me now, on a large plate of Ortigas de Mar, which the menu translated as 'Sea Nettles'. They are actually sea anemones, or the particular type of sea anemone that has its being off the coast of Conil. There was a strong hint of mucus about them and a certain amount of sand, but they smelt of the sea and that was enough for me. Having guzzled a plateful of the anemones we continued our journey to Cádiz without giving Conil even half a chance.

It seemed we missed a trick, for Conil really is a very pretty little town and we were in good spirits as we made our way to our tuna jurors' hotel. The woman at reception was German and her Spanish was not too good. Michael and I have only the shakiest of German between us. With some effort we managed to make her understand that we had been booked in by the Tourist Board. She looked at us suspiciously – perhaps thinking that we were about to try and sell her some ice cream. Eventually we established that a room had been booked for us. The budget was tight and so we had to share, but the good Dr Jacobs and I had over the years travelled together through Peru in conditions of the most outrageous intimacy, and a couple of nights in a Spanish seaside hotel without the privacy of individual rooms would do us no more harm.

'Dere iss a liff if you vont,' said the woman, giving us a look of distaste.

'I beg your pardon?'

'You zimmer iss on der firs flor; if you vont dere iss a liff to go upp.'

I stared at Michael and Michael stared back at me, then we both stared at the German woman with our mouths open. Just how bloody decrepit did she think we were? Michael glowered at the woman and stumped up the stairs. I glowered at her in turn but decided to take the lift; that would teach her. There was a mirror in the lift. Michael was right – I looked like an old, gay ice-cream salesman.

★   ★   ★

That night we were to dine as guests of the Conil Tourist Board, with Pepa and Mari-Carmen, who were its head honchos. We were the only jurors in town; the others would turn up on the day of the event itself, not having the long journey that the doctor and I had undertaken. We met the women at the hotel bar and kissed one another chastely on the cheek, and then, because I thought it was amusing and might break what little ice was there to break, I went into the ice-cream salesman routine and told our hostesses what Michael had said about my beautiful jacket. They averred, both of them, that it was a very fine jacket, if not perhaps the very apex of current fashion. These were young women and they knew what they were talking about in the fashion department; I felt vindicated.

We crammed into Pepa's tiny car, the doctor and I in the back, grasshopper-like, with our knees up by our ears, and headed out of town in order that nobody could get at us, and, by means of skulduggery, influence the result of the competition. The important thing, obviously, was to keep us out of the clutches of Cuqui and thus avoid any possible accusation of malfeasance. We were to eat at a restaurant that, for reasons of its own, had decided not to enter the running. I suggested to our hostesses, in what I thought was a humorous way, that perhaps this might be because it was not up to the mark on the gastronomy front.

'Judge for yourself,' said Mari-Carmen a little tartly.

Everybody made a great fuss of us as we were introduced to the owner, the chef and the waiters. The place was just the way I like my fish restaurants to be: on the beach so you could wiggle your toes appreciatively in the sand, and with a nice blue nautical theme – nets and knots and old anchors, lobster pots and other bits of fishing gear propped up here and there. I could see that the doctor thought it a little corny, but I felt it was perfect. And the fish . . .

'Would a selection of tuna dishes chosen by myself be acceptable?' asked the owner unctuously. I think he thought that Michael and I were more serious *gastrónomos* than we actually are. We all found this suggestion most amenable and sat down amidst a flurry of fussing and mussing from the waiters. Now, when I say tuna you may be thinking of that dry cardboard-like tuna that comes in tins; actually fresh tuna, and certainly the sort of fresh tuna that was doing the rounds in Conil at *almadraba* time, is something quite different. A tuna is a big fish: it can weigh up to half a ton, and there are many different cuts, and many of those cuts are the most tender, succulent, toothsome morsels you could ever imagine.

White wine from a vineyard down the coast was brought and poured ice cold into great balloons of crystal, and after they had given suitable time to Michael and my jokes and banter, Mari-Carmen and Pepa launched into the *almadraba* spiel. Conil, they told us, and its neighbour, Barbate, down the

115

coast, had been fishing tuna since way before the Romans. Maybe even in the time of the Phoenicians. The Romans made 'garum' from the fermented guts of the fish, and this, a concoction very much like 'Gentleman's Relish', was exported all over the Mediterranean. The general lack of enthusiasm in the modern world for a sauce made from fermented fish guts has brought the garum trade to an end, but the tuna fishing continues and arouses high passions.

Most tuna, these days, is swept up by an industrial fleet that ravishes the oceans in search of ever greater profit, heedless of any consequence. The *almadraba*, although unlikely to arouse the enthusiasm of the tuna themselves – for fish slaughtering by any means is a pretty unedifying business – takes a small toll of the fish stocks, using manpower from the coastal towns and a cunningly contrived system of nets to entrap a portion of the spring and autumn migrations of tuna. There are quotas, too, and it would seem that the draconian imposition of these over recent years is resulting in a slight revival of stocks. This year's quota, so we were told, was filled in record time.

My aquarium-builder friend Simon, who knows about tuna, having set up an education project at Palma de Mallorca, insists that we should not eat any tuna at all – not skipjack, nor yellowfin, nor bluefin, nor red – if we want our grandchildren to enjoy these fish in the seas and on the table. The species is that close to extinction. He does concede, though, that you may be able to justify eating an appetiser or two of tuna caught by sustainable means of fishing, like the *almadraba*. With this bit of sophistry I was able to ease my conscience enough to tuck in to the dainty morsels brought that night for our delectation.

Simon it was, too, who told me that we shouldn't eat octopus. It wasn't that they are in danger of extinction, but the fact that they are so advanced along the evolutionary scale that they love beauty. Apparently they create gardens at the mouths of their caves on the sea floor, amusing themselves by making pleasing arrangements of shells, fish-bones and bottletops and suchlike. 'How can you eat a creature that loves beauty?' he would admonish me.

For years, accordingly, I denied myself the pleasure of eating octopus, and whenever I found myself in a *pulpería* – which was not that often, as the reason for visiting a *pulpería*, as the name would imply (*pulpo* means 'octopus'), is to eat octopus – I would upbraid the owner on the ills of his trade. My stance did not win me friends in that part of the community. And then one day I was passionately holding forth upon the beastliness of eating octopus, when my interlocutor stopped me with an incredulous look, saying, 'Octopus! But they are the *hijos de putas* – the sons of bitches – who eat the baby turtles!'

I told all this to Pepa and Mari-Carmen, who

were not much impressed; they clearly wanted to tell us more about their tuna. About ten years before, with the tuna catch dwindling and the fortunes of the town ailing, somebody came up with the idea of setting up a tuna-cooking competition among the local restaurants. It coincided with the spring tuna harvest, and used the first fat and succulent tuna of the year. The *concurso* was a tremendous success in fettling up the cookery on offer and encouraging gastronomical tourism. From small beginnings it had now grown so that no fewer than thirty-three restaurants took part.

Thirty-three restaurants. I did a swift calculation as I embarked eagerly upon the evening's fourth exquisite dish of tuna. Thirty-three entrants would mean at least thirty-three different dishes to taste and judge. I looked darkly at the Doctor, whose eyes were shut, his face suffused with gastronomic ecstasy.

'Michael, do you know what this means?'

'Do I know what what means?' he mumbled absently.

'There are no fewer than thirty-three entrants in this *concurso*.'

'So? I f-fail to see what you're driving at.'

'Well, according to my calculations that means that we are going to eat thirty-three different tuna dishes . . .'

'Of course. It's actually forty. I will be judging seventeen dishes, and you and your jury twenty-three.'

'But that's impossible,' I spluttered. 'You can't keep your critical faculties working for twenty-three different dishes.'

'It'll be *pan comido*,' said the Doctor, infuriatingly. 'I once had to judge a cherry brandy competition in Castillo de Locubín. I had to taste fifty brandies . . . and the best of them was truly disgusting. At the end of it I was catatonic.'

This information did little to allay my concern.

'You don't have to eat the whole dish, you know,' he continued. 'Just a morsel here, a morsel there . . . In Castillo de Locubín I didn't drink fifty whole glasses of cherry brandy. L-lord, no. I just took a sip from each one.'

It was alright for Michael, I reflected; he did this sort of thing all the time; but I wasn't sure if I would be able to think and speak critically about twenty-three morsels of tuna dishes. It seemed to me that the odds would be heavily stacked in favour of whoever was fortunate enough to be the first to present their offering. At the beginning of the *concurso* we jurors would be eager to fall upon the food, and the most mediocre of morsels would hit us where it counts. Later, as our bellies began to fill, the general enthusiasm would wane, until, towards the end, one would die rather than look at another tuna dish. I suppose the professional gastronome is able, through long and diligent practice, to take into account this inherent unfairness.

These, then, were my thoughts as I worked my

way through a fifth exquisite preparation of tuna. Perhaps it had not been such a good idea to eat tuna the night before the *concurso*. But this was Conil in *almadraba* time.

Eventually the wonderful meal was over and Pepa and Mari-Carmen dropped us back in town. It was about one in the morning by now, on a warm night. Turning a corner in the maze of the town, we came across a long table surrounded by late-night revellers.

'Cuqui!' cried Michael. 'Fancy seeing you here . . .'

And there, by the strangest of coincidences, was Cuqui, holding forth amongst her friends, a glass of wine in her hand. I had not met Cuqui before. We kissed our greetings. A glass of wine appeared, and a *tapa* of . . . yes, tuna.

Cuqui was an attractive, powerful woman, the sort you might encounter striding with the wind in her hair at the head of a multitude of triumphant workers, a club-hammer or sickle in hand. She was dressed in chef's whites, having just come off a shift at her restaurant, La Mejorana. I had been thinking that perhaps the best strategy to deal with the forthcoming ordeal would be to go to bed early with a good book, but this was not the Doctor's modus operandi, so we settled in for one of those long late-night sessions. And hey, sitting in the street in a pretty little seaside town on a warm night in May with good wine and good company . . . well, there are worse ways to spend one's time.

About three rounds into the early hours of the morning the little gathering broke up. Jesús, who was Cuqui's partner, offered to take us to a couple of bars he knew. The Doctor's face lit up. 'Well, alright, Michael, but just one drink in one bar,' I insisted. So we sat in the square and drank super-strength *cuba libres* while Jesús and Cuqui debated which clubs we might move on to, to prolong our night's revelry.

After a little while – I'm not a fan of *cuba libres* – which in Spain cover everything fizzy with spirits, from gin and tonic to the deeply aberrant whisky and coke – I made my excuses and walked back to the hotel. There I coasted along the shores of sleep, haunted by visions of groaning mounds of tuna, Pepa and Mari-Carmen egging me on to ever more frightful feats of gluttony. Then at last I swam thankfully into the net and drifted lazily into the sweet bower of slumber.

Suddenly the door crashed open, and with a foul oath the Doctor stumbled into the room.

'YOU AWAKE STILL, CHRIS? You really missed something: we went to the most wonderful bar. I think it was the best bar I have ever been in.'

'I thought that was in Medina Sidonia,' I groaned, 'and I was asleep, as it happens. I was dreaming that I was a tuna swimming into the *almadraba* net.'

'Well you b-better get out of there a bit quick; we've got a lot of tuna to eat tomorrow. Time to get some sleep.'

He stomped from the room and proceeded to lay waste to the bathroom; the oaths and the thrashing about and the rushing of turbulent waters sounded like nothing so much as an *alma-draba*. Then he hurled himself onto his bed and within thirty seconds was snoring loudly. I inserted my ear-plugs and reflected that you would have to like somebody like Michael an awful lot to go travelling with them.

The gathering round the table in the street had impressed upon me the serious nature of our task. A great deal of hope and investment in effort and time had gone into the *concurso* and I resolved to play my part. Accordingly, next morning I woke the Doctor early, and after a light breakfast, took him for a long brisk walk along the beach. Other people were walking their dogs, flirting with the idea of going in the water – 'The Atlantic Ocean in May!' shuddered Michael – or combing the sand with metal detectors, looking, so they told us, for coins and jewels dropped from people's pockets. We strode barefoot and with our trouser legs rolled up, like gay ice-cream salesmen, beneath the invisible nylon lines of fishermen fishing from the beach. We peered sympathetically into their empty buckets.

Half a kilometre off the beach were the buoys of the *almadraba* nets. We wondered that the tuna would swim so far inshore when there was the whole of the strait at their disposal. 'I expect it's because of the currents,' I informed Michael. 'There'll be eddies along the shore that they can swim with, whereas they would be pushed to make headway against the massive bodies of water moving through the centre of the straits.' I stopped for a minute to marvel at this perspicacious piece of deduction.

The sun was getting higher and the heat of the day was starting to make itself felt. 'We'd better be getting along,' said Michael, 'it's quarter-past eleven and the *c-concurso* k-kicks off at half-past.'

Half-past eleven seemed cruelly early for a gastronomic *concurso*. I wasn't in the least bit hungry. But we scuffed the sand from our feet on the boardwalk, slipped into our shoes and walked up to the Escuela de Hostelería to our fearful task. I felt just the littlest bit sick.

The place was already packed out. There was a patio all decked up for festivity with a lot of umbrellas and chairs brightly emblazoned with a brewery logo; there was a *venencero* – one of those coves who, dressed in medieval costume, miraculously dispenses sherry from a barrel with a silver cup on the end of a long whippy cane; and there was a free bar. Things were shaping up nicely and the Doctor and I began to feel more positive about the coming ordeal. We glided through the already raucous throng, smiling and nodding benignly – although clearly nobody had the faintest idea who we were – towards the bar.

There we were both grasped firmly from behind. Our captors were Pepa and Mari-Carmen.

'Oh no, you don't,' they said, almost in chorus.

'D-don't w-what? . . .' stammered the Doctor and I in unison, a little taken aback.

'You mustn't mingle with the general public. If we let you in there, who knows what might happen to you? And you mustn't drink. Jurors drink only water.'

'W-water!?' blubbered the Doc, incredulous. 'We can't drink water . . . water drowns the taste buds; it stupefies the palate, distends the belly. It oxidises the critical faculties, dilutes acuity. You wouldn't wish it on your worst enemy.'

But Pepa and Mari-Carmen were having none of it. They steered us to an enclosure separated from the patio and its public by the thinnest of screens, where two big round tables were set with heaps of gleaming cutlery, napkins, and bottles of water. We were the only people in there. We looked at one another in dismay; coming through the thin screen was the sound of corks popping, the jolly clink of glasses and the infinitesimal hiss of the fine golden stream of sherry arcing through the air to land sizzling in the glass as the *venencero* did his spectacular stuff. All the glorious sounds of wine and fiesta.

'A nice glass of water, Michael?' I suggested. 'Get us in the mood . . .'

We sipped the clear liquid and took stock of our inner sanctum. We were right next to the kitchen, and through glass panels in the doors we could see a sort of infernal lobster quadrille as the white-clad chefs and the black-clad waiters bobbed and weaved and dipped and hurtled about amongst the jets of steam, raging fires and clashing knives.

Our fellow jurors began to drift in. First was Danny, an enormous, jolly young man with a goatee beard. He was a chef and owned a chain of restaurants on the Cádiz coast. You only had to look at him to realise that he knew his stuff in the cookery department. Next there appeared a couple of the smoothest, snappiest-dressed young men from Sevilla. The Doctor had them down instantly as *pijos*, or toffs. They were improbably handsome, slim, tanned and exquisitely groomed, but you couldn't hold this against them for long because they were disarmingly charming. One of them, Nicolás, was president of the Ibero-American Gastronomic Society, or some such thing, and between them, as a sort of hobby, they ran a charity for street kids in Cuba. I started to feel a little relieved that I was not to be president of this august gathering.

To make us up to the two sets of four jurors, there was a bouncy sort of a food journalist and a couple of other blokes who said they were food critics, but whose reason for being there was clearly as nebulous as Michael's and mine. Who is *not* a food critic, after all? We all bobbed and bowed and introduced ourselves and poured one another libations of water. It has to be said, though, that things were not going down with a bang at this

125

stage. It felt like a convention of abstainers and made you realise just what a help a bit of hooch is on these occasions. To exacerbate the awfulness of this situation, the odd dignitary was ushered in to shake our hands and come up with a platitude or two, and then there were the inevitable photographs of us all grinning at one another over our hateful glasses of water. Beyond the screen, of course, the merrymaking was notching fast up the scale as the beer and wine did their stuff.

And then suddenly the kitchen doors burst asunder and a slinky, black-clad waitress emerged and placed the first dish on the table. Beside it she put a number and the description of the dish, but no indication of which chef or which restaurant. At the same time an identical dish was taken out for the delectation of the public; they couldn't eat it – just look at it. They had the benefit of the name of the restaurant, and of course some wine. We could hear a lot of oohing and aahing as the public considered dish #1.

Dish #1 looked pretty good and it was one of ours – *cocina tradicional*. It was, according to the card, and if my memory serves me well *Parpatana de atún rojo al 10rf con couscous de frutos secos y torrija salada*. It was served on a particularly pleasing blue platter, clearly handmade by a local potter. A nice touch, I thought. We four jurors of *cocina tradicional* considered the dish earnestly. Michael and the other jurors of *cocina innovadora* came over to consider it, too, as their first dish

126

had not arrived and they were hungry and keen as mustard to get going.

We all murmured in the way that gastronomes do as we assessed the dish for the first category on our check-list: appearance and presentation. The thing was art itself, exquisitely composed and conceived to gladden the heart and quicken the taste buds. I was instantly ravenous.

'Shame about the platter,' said Nicolás. 'Tuna should never be served on anything but white plates. The blue makes it look grey and unappetising.'

He did not offer this as a suggestion – it was a fact.

Everybody agreed enthusiastically, though I kept my own counsel. I still liked the blue plate . . . but of course I could see that white might have enhanced the look of the dish a little better. There were five categories: presentation, taste and texture, ingredients, technical skill and authenticity, and five points was the maximum for each. I took up my scorecard and pen and gave it four. Actually, I figured the presentation was worth a five, but I didn't want to look too much of a fool. Weak and vacillating of me, I know . . . but if I can muster an excuse it's that I was a little unsure as to my qualifications for inclusion on this jury. I cook a little, and enjoy good food, but I'm not the sort of chap who over the years has eaten scores of, say, *Parpatana de atún rojo al 10rf con cous-cous de frutos secos y torrija salada*, and assessed the merits of each. And, as for its authenticity . . . well, I gave it five; the cook knew a lot more than I did about authenticity. Quality of ingredients, too: I figured you'd be a fool to enter a dish in a cookery contest and use a week-old fish, second-rate ingredients, so I gave all the ingredients a five.

Then at last came the moment we were all waiting for. The tasting.

The fabulous-looking *parpatana* sat on its inappropriate blue platter in the centre of the large round table. We, the jurors, stood around the table, bobbing and jostling to and fro as we considered the dish from different angles. Some were taking photos of the dish with their mobile phones. Finally, we had seen enough and it was time to demolish the exquisitely crafted composition . . . and eat it.

With our forks we lunged for the centre of the table and speared first a piece of *parpatana* – oh, Jeezus, it was the most heavenly thing that had ever passed my lips – then a pinch of the nutty couscous – the word 'divine' came to mind – and finally we cut up the savoury *torrija* toast and each conveyed a little piece to our mouths. Words started to fail me. I was ecstatic; the dish was a masterpiece. I reached for my card and gave it the maximum five points for flavour and texture. As for technical skill, well, obviously another five. It was looking good for dish #1: a four and four fives. I looked at it and felt a bit bad about the four, so I put in a little plus sign by the five for taste and texture. Perhaps I could reassess when we reached the end. To remind me, I added a little arrow going up.

The end, though, was a long way off. We had just eaten the first dish and all my superlatives were exhausted. There remained twenty-two offerings to follow. Lord knows where things were going to go.

After Nicolás and me and the food critic and the bouncy journalist had had our fill, there was not much left on the plate. The scrapings were cleaned up by Michael's jury, who left the plate absolutely bare. 'Just getting into the swing of the thing,' they said.

Then the first dish of *cocina innovadora* arrived. The very sight of it made us gasp as one: *Raviolis de ventresca de atún y puerros con esferificación natural de salicornia y aire de limón*. We all gravitated to the innovators' table, our forks twitching apprehensively, waiting for the jury to finish their appraisal of the presentation, and after the innovative jurors had done their stuff we all fell upon those ravioli as one, licking our lips and groaning with delight. Not a stitch, nor a stain, remained on the plate. I had never eaten such food.

We all took congratulatory sips of water.

Next up, dish #3, was another conventional: *Filetitos de atún a la menier con escalibada de la huerta de Conil*. We all looked at it for a bit; it looked good. A five, I thought.

'Hurry up,' said Danny the Chef. 'Our next plate is about to come.'

Once again we conventional jurors attacked the composition, followed eagerly and definitively by the innovators. It was incomparably delicious. Five . . . with a little plus sign by it. I furtively added another plus sign to the *parpatana*. As for the technique, well it was flawless: there was just enough moistness, just enough crunch – another five. Five for ingredients: it was a fresh fish and the vegetables were excellent . . . And five for authenticity, obviously. Hmm . . . that made five fives. It was certainly good, but it was no better than the *parpatana*; and what if there were better concoctions to come? Surreptitiously I added a squiggly arrow pointing down, and then, as an aide-mémoire an R and an L, meaning 'Reappraise Later'.

The tide of jurors, *convencionales* and *innovativos*, sloshed back to the other table to check out the next innovative offering. Each man – for we were all men – brandished his cutlery, his glass of water and his mobile telephone. This time it was that old favourite, *Tarantelo de atún braseado sobre lecho de cocochas napado con salsa suave de atún* . . . where *tarantelo* is the side of the tuna beneath the *lomo* and the *solomillo*, while a *lecho de cocochas* is a bed of cheeks, probably tuna cheeks in this case, all topped off with a suave sauce of tuna. Most of these terms don't appear in the dictionary, though, so if the truth be told it was anybody's guess.

The dish was certainly a looker, an opinion shared by most of us, judging from the gasps of amazement and admiration. The pens scribbled on the scorecards, then the forks massacred the delicate balance of the presentation and we were wreathed for a bit in critical murmurings of approbation or disdain. The edge of our ravenous appetites was slightly dulled by this time and it was more a matter of poking about and nibbling, rather than the voracious devouring that had gone before. It still tasted pretty good – straight fives in my opinion – but then so had everything.

I looked over at the Doctor, giving him a grin of collusion. He had a glass of fino – dry sherry – in his hand. He grinned back. And then I saw that all the innovators were drinking fino. Danny the Chef, it appeared, had called for wine to sharpen the innovators' dwindling senses, and his call had been heeded and wine produced. We, the conventionals, were racked with indignation, until within a minute or so there were a couple of bottles of sherry on our table, too. Things were looking up again. The slight decline in our enthusiasms, engendered by the inordinate piggery with which we had treated the first four dishes, returned instantly to a gastronomic euphoria. Now, instead of sousing ourselves with water, we could hone our senses to the sharpest pitch by steeping them in the pale gold nectar of a Manzanilla. We jurors slapped one another manfully on the back and bent our shoulders to the wheel; only thirty-six more dishes to go . . .

Dishes #5 and #6, which followed the introduction of the sherry, were greeted with howls of unanimous acclaim. More straight fives on my scorecard. There were a lot of straight fives on my scorecard, I reflected, albeit fives mitigated and modulated by a lot of unfathomable arrows, pluses and minuses, random letters, and other less familiar mathematical symbols. The scorecard was starting already to look a bit like the theory of relativity.

The food was just so good; I had never eaten anything quite like it, and as a consequence my critical faculties were reduced to ecstatic exclamations. Straight five continued to follow straight five. Later an unfortunate oversight, where some bleach had tainted one of the dishes, caused me to drop it down to a three for taste. Bleach tastes detestable, but even there the glorious taste of the tuna shone through. But then I felt sorry for the cook whose hopes had been dashed by somebody's failure to rinse the plate properly, so I added a couple of pluses, an ascending arrow and a ≤ sign, and then a few annotations. 'JABOB' it said, which I could only assume when I looked at it later meant 'Just A Bit Of Bleach'.

The dishes kept on coming, and as each jury passed the ten mark, more bottles of fino were called for to rouse our flagging spirits. No longer were we wolfing down the leftovers of the innovators, nor were they besieging our table for the scraps of conventionality. Indeed, the wolfing had turned to pecking. The immaculate tablecloths and napkins were thickly caked in the droppings from our unsteady forks and it was getting hard to find a place for the food for the heaps of bottles arrayed upon the tables. My back and hip were aching from all that bobbing about and bending half over, and there was a feeling of slight biliousness creeping upon me. The cooking was still world-class, but I was beginning to wish I wasn't here.

Our eleventh dish was the inevitable *Atún con chocolate*. I was not sure I could face it. I had to say it looked a lot better than you would expect of such unpromising bedfellows, though I gave it four for presentation because there was a small smear of chocolate where I didn't think there ought to be one. On the other hand, taste and texture were unquestionably excellent . . . so, five and some never-to-be-deciphered squiggles. Authenticity . . . hmm, I decided to award it four, but qualified by a question mark and a symbol that may have been a reference to the Incas.

The more temperate scores that now graced my scorecard were a consequence of several factors. First, a feeling that my undiluted enthusiasm, reflected in an unbroken procession of straight fives, was not going to get us far in choosing the winner – and a winner there had to be – this was, after all, a *concurso* and a *concurso* by its nature has a winner. Second, a slightly reduced enthusiasm for tuna, as a consequence of overexposure. As yet this diminishing had not gone as far as, say, never wanting to see another dish of tuna as long as I lived, but that was not unimaginable. And third, I had surreptitiously had a look at Danny the Chef's scorecard, which he had inadvertently left face up on the table as he poured everybody another slug of sherry. Danny the Chef, who as I have said before clearly knew his stuff when it came to the preparation of tuna, had carefully filled in his card with an eloquent array of ones and twos and threes.

By this time we were round about dish #13, and from there on a study of my scorecard reveals a more sober approach than the mindless enthusiasm that guided my judgement in the earlier stages of the competition. You might suggest that this is not fair, and of course it's not bloody fair, but such is the nature of these contests. You would have thought – as I had ventured earlier – that those who had the good fortune to present their offerings at the beginning would inevitably win, for there lies the logic . . . but, if you'll bear with me, events were to prove otherwise.

Although it was only May, it was hot, and hotter still in the jurors' enclosure, which was right beside the kitchen. The public outside, now really well oiled and reaching a pitch of anticipation, both for the results of the competition and, indeed, lunch, sounded like Armageddon. Those jurors who were wearing ties and jackets had taken them off, and a reeling sense of bonhomie, mixed with a growing nausea, prevailed.

Things calmed down noticeably with the arrival of conventional dish #14, the refreshingly unequivocal *Atún a la antigua* – tuna at the antique. I imagined, to my own hoots of private mirth, a large fish running amok amongst the Meissen and Ming. It was OK . . . I gave it a four, a couple of fives, a three and a two. This last, the lowest score on my card, was prompted by a swift look at Nicolás's card. He had given it a one, so I, who had been about to give it the customary five, dropped to the two. Then I felt bad about it because by this time I had forgotten what that particular category was about anyway, so I mitigated my disdain with another arrow pointing up.

Christ, there were another nine dishes to go. I was feeling distinctly queasy – and even my expert co-jurors were beginning to look a little green around the gills. I hazarded a guess that most of us had more or less lost our critical faculties at this point and were coasting along in survival mode, just hoping to get to the end without besmirching ourselves.

There was a hush . . . the kitchen door flew open . . . and in came innovative dish #15. We all gathered in dumbstruck silence to consider this outrageous offering. The dish was presented on a mirror; in a corner of the mirror was a rack containing three test tubes, two of which were filled with coloured liquid, while the third was full of swirling smoke. Nearby was a fine glass retort – looking much like one of those bottles you have to pee in when you can't get out of bed – which was full of lurid green liquid. A raised glass plate was arrayed with pieces of raw tuna and other indecipherable stuff, all disposed to resemble things that they were not, and the reflections of these in the mirror made the whole improbable composition even more bizarre. As a surreal creation it was fabulous, but how would one go about eating it? The innovators discussed this problem amongst themselves and, by judicious pouring and sniffing and sipping, found a way. And, in spite of the torpor that was overtaking all of us now, they pronounced that it was every bit as extraordinary to eat as it looked . . . and it looked like a winner.

Oh, how we envied the innovators, who now had only two dishes left to taste, whereas we had no fewer than nine more to go. The hot morning moved on to a hot afternoon as dish followed dish for us to eye up unenthusiastically and then peck at. The quality did not flag, and there was even a light dish – some sort of foam – that afforded us the briefest respite. And then finally, just when we knew we could take no more, the last conventional dish arrived on our table. Talk about the short straw . . . of course, the last entrant wouldn't stand a chance, given the bloated, cynical, bilious state in which we the jurors now found ourselves. We stared at the thing through dull fishy eyes, clutching our stomachs, burbling quietly to ourselves, and wishing to die.

What the hell was this? A simple boat of coarse china sat on the table. It was stacked with hot grey charcoal, and perched above the coals on lollipop sticks were eight unadorned cubes of tuna, sizzling in the heat.

It was perfection itself, and simplicity . . . and it was the winner, being the only dish of the day to get straight fives from all four jurors. The winner of the innovators was the crazy concoction with the test tubes.

'Lunch, anybody?' suggested some wag.

It was over; we had made it. We were released to mingle with the public and look at the display of all the dishes with the name of the chef and restaurant. Fortunately, perhaps, for our reputations, Cuqui – who turned out to have been responsible for that first dish, *Parpatana de atún rojo al 10rf con couscous de frutos secos y torrija salada* – did not win.

As the Doctor and I waddled back through the town, heading for the hotel for a siesta, we passed a tempting-looking ice-cream parlour. It was just what we needed and we both sat down and guzzled chocolate ice creams washed down with coffee.

Then we decided to go for a swim . . . perhaps, being composed largely of tuna by now, we felt an urge to get into their element. There was nobody else swimming – it was, after all, early May – and the inhabitants of the beach watched, appalled, as the two bloated, old, gay ice-cream salesmen stripped to their grutts and wobbled into the sea. Childishly excited as a consequence of our relief at having come through the ordeal, we played at being tuna.

At about nine o clock that night we hit the town again. We went straight to Cuqui's. She was expecting us at her tiny restaurant, La Mejorana. We sat in the street and drank wine and ate even more of the most exquisite tuna.

Next morning I was raring to go for the long drive back to Granada, with a break for breakfast in Medina Sidonia. But for some reason Medina Sidonia didn't appeal and we drove on by without the much-vaunted pig fat breakfast. Perhaps we'll stop in Medina Sidonia next time.

CHAPTER 9

CURES FOR SERPENTS

High in the Alpujarras, a four-hour walk uphill from our farm, through the wildest of mountain scenery, lies a village which is blessed by the presence of a *curandera*, which is to say something between a faith healer and a barefoot doctor.

As a nation dons the cloak of modern urban existence, such people and their ancient gifts tend to vanish, but in the Spanish countryside today the tradition of healers is very much alive. If anything, there has been a resurgence in recent decades, now that they can practise without persecution. In Franco's time, *curanderos* were frequently beaten and jailed by the Guardia Civil at the instigation of his henchman, the Church – who, typically, felt that the monopoly on miracles should be theirs alone.

Now, our local *curandera* was on my mind because I had just heard a story about a London journalist who had been on holiday in her village. The poor man suffered from eczema, and, hearing about the *curandera* and her particular gift for curing skin diseases, was intrigued enough to pay her a visit. Within three days she had cured his eczema, simply by stroking the affected part. Fascinated and impressed, and of course enormously relieved, he wrote the episode up in his column. This came to the notice of a man who was unfortunate enough to have shingles in, of all places, his eye. The doctors had told him that there was nothing they could do and he might as well get used to the idea of losing the eye. He made some enquiries and came to the Alpujarras, where, after three sessions with the *curandera*, the shingles simply disappeared.

Of course, there are plenty of stories like this, but they are not necessarily about healers in your own backyard, and it was the backyard aspect of the story that got me thinking. For I myself had been suffering from a skin complaint, albeit – unlike the journalist and his follower – neither shingles nor eczema. No, my complaint was of an altogether more delicate nature – and afflicted that part of my person of which we do not speak.

To put the matter bluntly, I had a horribly inflamed dick.

Like all the best medical conditions, mine had a good and chequered history. It began back in the mists of time, almost a quarter of a century ago, when I was fortunate enough to enjoy the favours of a lady whose name conveniently escapes me. During the course of a relationship that pertained more to the nether abdomen than to the heart, she inadvertently left me with a painful little memento.

She and I were far from the only people in history to whom this has happened, and I bear her no ill will. And the painful little something was of the sort that comes and goes; indeed, the doctor said that it would appear and disappear with ever less frequency until it vanished altogether. This it proceeded to do until suddenly, many years later, the whole thing flared up again, like a long-dormant volcano, causing acute tenderness and a nasty swelling that not only put paid to any notions of amorousness but made it difficult to walk.

I mentioned the problem one morning to my Dutch neighbour Bernardo, who suggested that I might have 'fallen prey to a wind-blown particle'. He then proceeded to show me a most villainous-looking infection on his ankle that had, apparently, blossomed from a tiny microbe blown there by the wind. The theory didn't seem entirely plausible but, given my rural and monogamous state, it was as good as any other. So off I went, with my bandy-legged gait, to the local clinic. There, the doctor studied the affected area with little enthusiasm and sent me home with a *pomada* – a cream – that I was to slap on three times a day. Not that it was certain to do me much good, he added discouragingly.

Having bought his lotion, I set to studying the list of *efectos secundarios* on the packet. 'Skin irritation', it began. Well, I was used to that, though it did seem out of the frying pan into the fire. 'Loss of appetite . . .' It didn't say what sort of appetite, but at my age you need all the appetite you can get. 'Nervousness . . . depression . . . chronic depression . . .' On and on it went.

It seemed manifestly unwise to apply this preparation to my person, particularly the more sensitive parts of it. So Ana consulted her herbal tomes and suggested the alternative of a saline solution.

This seemed innocuous enough, though you need a very strong solution. Seawater at 3.5 percent is not good enough, and even the 7 percent brine that you keep your olives in – the solution at which an egg floats to the surface – is not enough to deal with the maleficent microbes that can make life such a misery. No, to get those microbes scurrying for the hatches the solution must be no less than a ferocious 15 percent. For some days, morning and night, I applied this bestial solution to my person, and there was enough of a tang in it to make me feel that it was actually doing some good. But when I began to develop a sort of crystalline crust, not unlike the caramelised sugar on a toffee apple, it seemed wise to call a halt.

Next out of the natural medicine chest was an essential oil made from grapefruit pips. I applied this stuff daily, drop by drop, from the tiny bottle – but as a certain piquancy in the affected part started to become apparent, I belatedly consulted the label. Under no circumstances, it noted, should the product be applied neat. A dilution of 20:1 with almond oil or suchlike was recommended. By this time, the grapefruit seed oil had virtually flayed the flesh from my poor bone.

Finally, Ana came up with gentian violet. 'It says here', she announced, after another read of the herbal, 'that it's a gentle, uninvasive and surefire cure. I think we've got some gentian violet.' Which we did, though it was rather more than ten years past its sell-by date. 'Doesn't matter,' pronounced the wife. 'It's hardly going to go off, is it?'

What you do with gentian violet is drop a few drops in some water in a mug, and then hang the affected part in it for a bit. It has a gentle anti-bacterial action, though, if the truth be told, it didn't seem to do much good, beyond dyeing my penis a spectacular, deep and more or less indelible purple.

It was at this moment of despair that I came across the journalist's account of his trip. It was clearly my last and best hope.

I shillied and I shallied, and dithered a little, and then, after a few more days of bandy-legged agony, lunged for the telephone and rang the *curandera*.

'Speak,' she commanded. (This is what you say on the telephone in Spain.)

'Hello,' I said. 'Would you be the *curandera*?'

'Yes, that's me.'

'Well, I have a bit of a problem, and I was wondering if you might not be able to help me . . .'

'I'll do what I can. What is this problem?'

'It's a skin complaint . . .'

'That's what I do.'

'Yes, but . . . you see, well, it's on . . . I mean . . . what I'm saying is that . . .'

I had not rehearsed this as I ought to have done. I was digging a hole for myself and getting in deeper.

'You mean it's a penis, perhaps?'

'Well, in a sense, yes . . . it is a penis . . . er, do you do penises?'

'*Claro* – no problem. Can you come tomorrow?'

As it happened, we had friends arriving for a few days' holiday, but that was OK. This was a ball I wanted to get rolling. And after a great deal of thought, I decided to go on foot. Of course I could have taken the car and saved myself a lot of time. But that didn't feel right; it wouldn't have been portentous enough for an expedition of this nature. The *curandera* had told me that it wasn't necessary to be a believer, nor go to church, in order to benefit from her ministrations, but even so, I felt that any element of spirituality that I could enlist on my behalf could only help. And the very act of walking has a certain spiritual dimension – more than driving the car, at any rate.

And so, thus determined, I gathered the dogs, and, with hope in my heart and my complaint hanging heavily upon me, set off up the mountain. I decided to take the dogs along because, although spirituality is not exactly their thing, they do manifest joy and transmit it to their human companions

. . . and joy is a commodity of which one ought to take all one can possibly get.

As for the journey, well, placing one bandy leg in front of the other, time after thousands of times, and puffing and panting fit to burst my heart and lungs, I made headway through bright golden gorse and blue clouds of rosemary alive with diligent bees. I felt the elation that clambering amid mountains and raging rivers induces, and a tentative exuberance at the thought that I might soon be rid of my burdensome ailment . . . and also just a hint of apprehension. It was a complicated pot to keep on the boil.

Little by little I left the sounds of the valley below me, the roaring of the rivers swollen with winter rains, the sounds of cocks crowing and dogs barking. By the time I got to the *aljibe*, the stone-vaulted cistern that stands on the ridge between our valley and the next, there was nothing but the moaning of the wind in the broom. This is a sound of sinister portent, one that touches the darkest chords of our collective being.

I felt like a character in a Dennis Wheatley novel, the hapless protagonist in an imminent battle between the forces of good and evil. And things didn't improve as I entered the village and made my way, as instructed, past the spring, left at the end of the alley, and down to the last house on the left. I stood collecting myself for a minute before the green wooden door. From inside came the sound of children's laughter.

That didn't seem right; the last thing I needed now was children laughing . . . this was no laughing matter.

I thought for a minute of doing a bunk, calling the whole wretched thing off. I stood there vacillating, rocking back and forth, but then took heart and knocked hard on the door. The voices fell silent. Then a cry: 'It'll be your man.' The door opened and a woman peered out, dressed in floral housecoat and carpet slippers. She had an interesting and intelligent face and kindly eyes. 'Hello,' she said. 'Can I help you?'

'Er . . . I hope so . . . I'm the person with the . . . you know, I rang you yesterday . . .'

'Ah yes, you're Cristóbal. Don't mind all these people. Come inside.'

The door opened directly onto a small room, in the middle of which sat an incredibly aged woman in a straight-backed chair. 'This is América,' said the *curandera*, indicating the old lady, 'and this is Carmen.' Beside América stood a young hairdresser, making some adjustment to the few sparse strands of blue-grey hair that remained on the old lady's wrinkled head. The tableau was completed by a motley assortment of babies and children, scampering or crawling about the room, while a teenage boy sat in an armchair and glowered morosely.

At my entrance, the show seemed to have come to a stop: the scissors hovered motionless in the air while the hairdresser considered me with a bemused smile; the babies dribbled; the teenager offered me a sneer of dankest disdain; América looked me up and down with an expression of utter bafflement and increasing distaste, until all of a sudden she staggered half to her feet, opened her lipless old mouth and vomited copiously onto the cold tile floor.

I was hustled urgently through a door into a parlour and the door slammed behind me. I stood there alone, listening to the clattering of mops and buckets, the shrill cries of admonition to the children, the pitiful croaking of América.

The parlour was a whitewashed room – even the canes and beams were whitewashed – and I stood hesitantly next to a large TV until the *curandera* came in, pulling the door half-closed behind her. 'Poor old thing,' she said. 'She's ninety-five years old, you know.'

'I . . . I hope it wasn't my fault,' I ventured idiotically.

'What? The vomiting? Heavens, no! She does that all the time.'

She put her hands in the pockets of her housecoat and gazed at me in silence. I shifted my weight from one foot to the other and squinted back. After a bit she said: 'You're the one that wrote that book, aren't you?'

'Er . . . yes.'

'You live down there at El Valero, don't you? I know all about you. She flapped her housecoat. 'Now, what seems to be the problem?'

'It's my . . . er . . .' and I indicated my crotch.

'Alright, then,' she said. 'Out with the *culebrina* and let's have a look.' (A *culebrina* is a little serpent.)

This was it. I fumbled with the buttons of my fly, then bent over and reached in, gingerly coaxing the timid little creature from its lair for inspection. The *curandera* peered at it, aghast. It was not looking its best.

'It's a nice colour,' she observed after a bit. 'Don't you worry . . . we'll fix it up in no time.' And so saying, she sprinkled some talcum powder on the affected part, and set to rubbing it with a gentle circular motion.

This was far from unpleasant – in fact it felt really rather nice. I strove to think about something disagreeable in order to discourage any untoward tumescence. But try as I might, the thoughts wouldn't come. It was too nice a day: there was a beautiful low winter sun; I had enjoyed a long walk accompanied by joyful dogs to a lovely Alpujarran village; my penis was being rhythmically rubbed; and soon I would be walking back to a blazing fire and a delicious supper in the company of family and friends. I could feel blood creeping ominously about my body, looking for some empty space to fill, some erectile tissue perhaps, to make turgid . . . and turgid was the last thing I needed right now.

The *curandera* meanwhile was still rubbing. So I struggled to think of something dull and dispiriting. This of course is a tried and tested sexual technique; instead of meditating on, say,

148

the beauty and sinuousness of bodies, or silk knickers, music and wine – lines of enquiry that can easily bring things to too abrupt a head – one considers the Spanish predilection for acronyms, or the lamentable decline in whale stocks, or the curious relationship between a liquid's viscosity and its meniscus.

There are plenty of such things but it's sometimes hard to fish them out when you need one. However, there was a silver crucifix on top of the telly, and this put me in mind of the mines of Potosí in Bolivia. Now there are few topics better conceived to banish impure thoughts than the horrific treatment imposed by the *conquistadores* on the indigenous populations of South America. My coursing blood was instantly stilled.

'Can we talk?' I suggested, thinking to lower the tension by means of some banal conversation.

'Of course we can. What do you want to talk about?' The *curandera* applied a little more talc.

'You said that I don't have to be a believer to benefit . . .'

'No, no, not at all. It makes no difference. I've treated all sorts, all the local boys – and they're not believers, I can tell you. The doctor sends them straight to me nowadays; he knows there's nothing he can do.'

She went on to tell me how she first realised she had the 'gift'. At the age of nineteen she had felt compelled to stroke the skin of a baby who was suffering from a painful skin complaint: 'I don't know why; I just had this urge, so I asked the mother if I could hold the poor thing. I picked it up and stroked it where it was sore, and it stopped screaming. I went back every day, and by the end of the week it was healed . . . I've been doing it ever since, about forty years now, it must be. People bring me all sorts of things to cure . . .' She paused. 'And I've seen an awful lot of penises. There, that ought to be done now; you can put it away.'

I buttoned up thankfully while the *curandera* returned the talcum powder to its drawer.

'How does it feel now?' she asked.

'Well, I'd be lying if I said it was better, but that was very soothing, and I think it's less painful.' And I meant it.

'Come again tomorrow morning, but not too early.'

'It won't be that early; it took me four whole hours to walk here . . .'

'Walk? You didn't walk all the way from down there!'

'I did indeed.'

'What on earth for? Why not drive like any sane person?'

'Well I like walking, and . . . I thought it might be more appropriate for a thing of this nature, more . . . spiritual?'

'I've never heard such nonsense. Heavens, no. Bring the car tomorrow; it'll save you a lot of time.'

★　　★　　★

The next day I took the car. I wanted to be home for lunch, for one thing, and it meant I could take some gifts – home-made apricot jam, a sack of oranges and a bag of aubergines. The *curandera*'s village is too high for orange trees, and that year we had late aubergines.

After the third treatment, the inflammation had almost disappeared, and I asked how much I owed.

'Come and see me one more time in a week and we'll check that it's all over,' she said. 'And, as for the money, you don't owe me a thing. I don't do cures for money.'

'But. . . but,' I spluttered. 'Nobody does anything without money. Have you never taken money, then?'

'I've never really thought about it, but it's a gift, and it wouldn't seem right to accept money for it.'

I looked around the little room. The *curandera* was far from being a wealthy woman. She had told me that she took whatever work she could get: cooking, cleaning, grape and olive harvesting and suchlike.

A week later, the day of the final checkup, I rose in the very best of spirits. A cool winter sun was pouring from a cloudless sky, and there wasn't the slightest twinge of unpleasantness from my trousers. On such a day the only way to go was to walk, and I rocketed up the hill like a jack rabbit. Gone now the bandy-leggedness, no more the hoots of pain from the penis. There was a skip in my step as I entered the *curandera*'s village, where

I found her sitting on a bench in the sunshine, passing the time of day.

After a last brief session with the talcum powder, we agreed that my ailment was good and gone, and sat in the kitchen for a while exchanging aubergine recipes. I gave her some olive oil from the farm and a box of home-made quince jelly.

On the way back, the dogs skipped about in the scrub, visible only by their tails held high – and if I'd had a tail myself, I think I'd have wagged it right off. We were all feeling that good. And as we breasted the rise where the long descent into our valley begins, I stopped for a bit to admire the lowering rays of sunshine making shadows in the folds of the sierras. The gentlest evening breeze rose from the bowl of the valley. It was the time and place, I reckoned, for a leak.

I looked about me and sought out a plant that would benefit from a warm watering with nitrogen-rich, pathogen-free pee. A tiny, perfectly formed juniper bush presented itself and I gleefully soused the little plant, while a million billion infinitesimal wind-blown particles rose from the valley, bathing us in an invisible cloud . . . But what did I care? There was always the *curandera* up the river.

CHAPTER 10

MANUALIDADES

'Times are hard and getting harder,' said Manolo, idly crushing a beer can. 'People are eating cats.' It's hard to leave a statement like that hanging. I cracked a handful of almonds and looked him in the eyes.

'*Hombre*, how do you know that people are eating cats?'

'Because', Manolo explained slowly, 'Juan at the Venta was delivered a box of rabbits last week and four of them had no heads on.' He leaned back with an air of finality.

I considered the information aghast, though still a little bit baffled. Finally I could contain myself no longer. 'But what have headless rabbits got to do with the eating of cats, Manolo?' Ana was all ears too, and we both looked at Manolo quizzically as he took the floor.

'Everybody knows . . .' he intoned in the manner in which one might address a halfwit, '. . . everybody knows that a rabbit without a head on is in fact a cat . . . or was.' He regarded us with a smile of triumph hovering above his thick black winter beard. But we still didn't get it.

154

'Friends,' he continued patiently. 'A skinned rabbit looks exactly the same as a skinned cat except for the head – and that's because of the ears. Cats' ears are different from rabbits' ears,' and he looked at us in order to be sure that we were with him on this most basic of zoological points, 'but apart from that they're identical.'

I cracked another dozen almonds – crisp and clean, one stroke only with the hammer – and reflected that, cat-rabbits or not, Manolo was right: times in Spain are hard, and, as he says, getting harder. I was in a junk shop last month, and the owner told me that a man had brought in a pile of what was essentially valueless rubbish; nobody would have paid a penny for the lot. When the dealer told him this, he almost wept. 'But I need money,' he said. 'My family has nothing to eat.'

The catch-all (or catch-most) welfare system that exists in northern Europe has no equivalent in Spain: you pick up benefit for a certain period, depending upon how long you have worked, but it soon ends and you are thrown upon the mercy of family and friends. As I write, there are more than a million households in the country where nobody has work; there is absolutely no money coming in at all. It's hard to imagine of twenty-first-century Spain, but people are hungry.

I kept on cracking nuts. It was what we call the *Hora de Manualidades* – Handicraft Hour – the time that Manolo comes up for a drink at the end of the day's work. He enjoys a bit of company at

155

the end of the day because he usually works on his own, and manual farm work gets lonely. Manolo drinks beer and we drink a Turkish sort of tea; we neither of us drink beer, and five in the afternoon seems a little early to start on the wine.

Sometimes we sit for as much as an hour, chatting in a desultory sort of a way. Manolo, it has to be said, is not the world's greatest conversationalist, so when on the odd occasion we run out of subjects of mutual interest, we lapse into long and comfortable silences. We have found that these are more agreeable on both sides if we are engaged in some sort of activity, something that is compatible with the desultory drone of intermittent conversation . . . and, of course, it gets things done.

The most obvious *manualidad* is almond-cracking. I bring to the table a bucket of Marconas, my favourite almond, sweet, fat and easy to crack. I spread an old towel and a cracked piece of marble on the table, and take a hammer I keep specially for the purpose. I spill a heap of almonds on the table and we set to cracking them. In an hour Ana and I between us can do a kilo – and that's a lot of almonds. Afterwards I blanch them, slip the inner skin off, toast them and mix them with a little olive oil, ground salt and *pimentón*. I defy you to come up with a simpler or more delicious thing, and all it costs is our labour, because we happen to have our own Marcona trees.

It has to be said, though, that the constant crack of the hammer doesn't aid conversation. So sometimes Ana will do some sewing; I might find something broken to fix. At various times there is garlic to string, or onions or home-grown tobacco. Or there is the satisfying task of shucking *habas*, broad beans. We eat the tender young beans and put the pods in a bucket for the sheep, who love them, and at the end of the season get to eat the plants, too.

These are timeless farm activities. If you talk to the old folks of the Alpujarra about the way things were before modern times, they all remember gathering at *cortijos* to share the task of shucking or 'podding' *habas*, shucking maize, stringing garlic and peeling onions. After the *habas* were shucked, or the onions peeled, inevitably somebody would bring out a guitar or a mandolin and everybody would end up dancing on the roof in the moonlight . . . which upon not a few occasions would lead conveniently to that other pleasurable cooperative activity of getting together to fix a broken roof.

I don't wish to appear too cynical about this, as the idea of dancing by moonlight on a flat roof in the remoter fastnesses of the Alpujarras to the sound of a mandolin, after a long hard day of *habas*-shucking, is about as romantic a thing as I can think of. And life in rural Spain, as we know, was unbelievably hard back then; there were few luxuries, and the idea of being delicate about eating would not have been well considered. Which perhaps explains the pained expression that Manolo adopted when we took to the somewhat refined *manualidad* of 'double-podding' *habas*.

Now, this is an activity that seems almost wilfully wasteful of time – *'una mariconada'* (an unmanly frippery), as Manolo pronounced it the first time I set to the task. However, I'm not so sure. As everybody knows, unless you pick it very early in its life cycle, the broad bean has a detestable flavour, like overcooked liver; it dries the mouth and leaves the palate with a disgusting after taste. The reason for this is the bean's coarse, grey-green outer skin. If, however, you blanch your *habas* for a couple of minutes, and then proceed to slip them out of their skins, you get the most exquisitely delectable food – bright green, tender and deliciously flavoured. It's a lot of work, and a bit boring . . . but it takes only seventeen minutes to prepare enough for four servings.

It's much like the business of squeezing *altramuces* out of their skins and into your mouth, and people pay good money for that. *Altramuces* are curious yellow beans with no flavour that are unaccountably popular as a *tapa* in Sevilla. The technique is to squeeze them with your fingers and let the inner part of the bean shoot into your mouth, leaving the outer skin between your fingers. It's a dish, and an activity, that wears thin very quickly . . . unless you happen to be from Sevilla.

*   *   *

The whole broad bean business had particular relevance that year, as Manolo, for some reason known only to himself, had sown about half an acre of *habas*, and we had had the most successful crop I had ever seen. *Habas* do well here, and it's the staple diet during the earlier part of the year. But even in this bumper year, when we could have picked every bean in its tiny delectable state, we found ourselves double-podding, for Ana insisted we pick the horrible old coarse ones first – so as not to waste them. What this means, of course, is that by the time you have got through the big horrible ones, the thin tender sweet ones have all in their turn become fat and horrible. It's the same with the raspberries, later on. Ana insists we eat the over-ripe fruit before we're allowed to get at the nice juicy fresh ones. By the time we get round to picking them they are rotten, too, so we only get to eat rotten raspberries . . . just like the 'orrible 'abbers. It's a deeply flawed system.

But to return to the task in hand. Before the second shucking of the *habas*, you have to get the beans out of their big pod. Ths is not unpleasant work and you can get through it tolerably quickly. But Ana considers it one of those jobs that must be combined with other activity, and, outside of our hour with Manolo, the best activity to combine it with is listening to audiobooks. Again I'm a little ambivalent about this as I have a sneaking, fastidious sort of a suspicion that I am detracting from the meaningfulness of both activities by combining them. However, that spring we had sackloads of *habas* to shuck, and so we both settled down with a bowl between our knees and headphones on our heads. You may perhaps wonder why we could not listen to the book together, as would seem to be logical. This was because, although we were listening to the same book (*The Heart is a Lonely Hunter* by Carson McCullers . . . and I defy you to come up with a finer novel), we were at different stages of it, on account of my having snaffled a couple of tapes to take on a car journey to Granada. I was therefore way ahead of Ana and as I didn't want to hear the earlier bits all over again, and she didn't want to skip any of the intevening parts, we had to resort to separate audio equipment.

So imagine us, if you will, of an evening, me sitting on the pouff, the Wife on the sofa, both engrossed in the story being read separately to us. Between us the bucket of unshucked *habas* was diminishing slowly, while the piles of podded beans in the bowls between our respective knees grew at an equal rate. Our faces were rapt in earnest concentration, except for every now and then when one or other of us would have a comment to make, more often than not upon the size or shape of some spectacular pod.

Ana would kick me and, as I looked up, signal to me to turn off my little tape player. I would fumble at the controls and eventually achieve this simple task. Then I would take the headphones

160

off and look at her expectantly. She had already gone through similar motions. Then she would hold up a bean. 'Look at this one,' she would say. 'How about that for a big bean?' I would chuckle obligingly and, having ascertained that she didn't want to comment any further upon the morphology of the bean in question, would return to my tape . . . until several minutes later I too might find myself sufficiently moved by the shape of a bean to want to put the whole process in motion again.

Of course, this procedure detracts to a certain extent from the sense of continuity of the book . . . it's as I said, I'm not sure it's the right thing to do. And when I think of those Alpujarreños of old sitting round together shucking *habas* and talking by the light of the fire, waiting for the moon and the mandolin . . . well, I know what they mean, those old folks, when they say they reckon that we have lost something.

CHAPTER 11

THE RAIN IN SPAIN

The locals say that it is autumn rains that do the most damage. The sweet showers of the new year seep lightly into the earth to nourish the shallow-rooted spring flowers, making the country glorious with colour and scent. But autumn rains, falling, as they sometimes do in this steep country, in opaque and thunderous sheets, can flay the daylights out of the land. The shaly earth, lashed by a merciless barrage, crumbles and dissolves, forming grey rivulets that snake into ever greater rivulets. And the greater rivulets become torrents and cascades, tearing the sodden land into gullies and chasms, abysses and gorges. At which point the water, now thick and grey and slow-moving, with the sludge it has gathered in its headlong downhill rush, pours, along with a hundred thousand other torrents, into the mother of all torrents: the river.

Spain, of course, with the exception of lush and sodden Galicia in the Atlantic northwest, is a country racked with droughts. And the southeastern quadrant of the Peninsula, which includes Almería, Murcia and our own province of Granada, is probably the driest part of Europe, with a rainfall not much greater than that of the Sahara Desert. And, although the following statement tends rather to the emotional than the statistical, of these driest parts of the dry, the driest of all is where we have chosen to make our stand: the Alpujarra. In fact it is only the presence of the snows on the peaks, and the aquifers beneath the Sierra Nevada, and the beautiful and intricate systems of irrigation devised by the Romans and the Moors, that keep our lush green valleys from becoming desert.

We often feel that we're living on the edge, on the delicately balanced frontier of a changing climate. The mean annual temperature in the Peninsula has been higher these last few years than since the records began in about 1850, and not a winter passes without the violence of the weather causing mayhem and fatalities in some part of the country. Sometimes there's a warning, a vision of the way things might go. In 1995, for instance, the year scheduled for the World Downhill Skiing Championships on the Sierra Nevada, there fell not a flake of snow, and the event had to be postponed for a year. The old boys who while away their days sitting at the entrances to the villages came out in force to announce that never before had such a thing been seen. Everybody shook their heads and, with earnest looks, predicted cataclysm and doom, although it has to be admitted that these are scenarios much discussed and enjoyed in the Alpujarra. Throughout the whole of that winter there was no rain and no snow, but in the summer, through the miracle of those bountiful aquifers, the springs and rivers kept on flowing. In 1996, it rained well and there was a thick cap of snow on the mountains.

So you never really know. Except in summer, when you can be fairly certain that between May and September you will have an unbroken succession of cloudless days, the weather in Andalucía does more or less what it will. '*¡Ay qué calor!*' the Spanish groan, even when it's not really that hot at all. The English may admit to a dull fascination with the weather, but the Spanish border on the obsessive in their weather commentary, which is an odd thing, since in summer every day is a cloudless day and the sun beats on down as predictably as ever.

After the agony of August is over, the first thing one does at the start of each day is scan the sky for sight of a cloud, that first harbinger of blessed rain. This is an activity fraught with frustration. The great black cloudbanks roll in from the west, spun off the mid-Atlantic lows, and usually spill their rain over Portugal, Huelva and Cádiz; Málaga might benefit from the last drops, but by the time they loom over us they're all bluster, dry as a bone. It's the hardest thing to bear when you're desperate for rain, those clouds seemingly charged with moisture.

And so it was, in Chloé's second year at college, that September crept in dry as a cracked stick, and it didn't rain in October either. Even in November it only registered a couple of litres, according to

Domingo's rain gauge – a wheelbarrow whose dimensions, he reckons, roughly correspond to the required square metre. (This is the way that rainfall is measured in Spain: the litres that fall upon a square metre.) Halfway up the side of the barrow, at roughly the point where fifteen litres would fill it, depending of course on the levelness, or other-wise, of the ground upon which the barrow is parked, is a small hole that releases water at a known rate, increasing with the rise in pressure as the water approaches the top and thus the awesome maximum capacity of the device. The unlettered Domingo, who is a person much given to such abstruse calculations, knows exactly how to calcu-late the sliding scale of water loss.

We have a rain gauge, too, a green plastic cone with a short spike in the bottom to stick in the earth. If it rains too much, it gets top-heavy and falls over in the wet mud. It's a cheap bit of kit, made of poor quality brittle plastic and poorly cali-brated; but if we wanted a proper quality rain gauge, we would have to shell out about a hundred and forty euros, which seems like an awful lot of money to pay for a calibrated plastic cone. Of course we're talking about a professional rain gauge here; if you wanted to submit your findings to some learnèd body, then this is what you would have to have. And besides, you would have to be the sort of person who would be prepared to commit himself to getting up early in the morning – because for some unfathomable reason these sorts of things always have to be done early in the morning – at the same time every day on all the days of the year, read your rain gauge and send off the fruits of your investigations to the learned body.

Now I know that this is the way that we humans and our society achieve excellence and progress: by assiduousness and scrupulous attention to detail, and fortunately there are heaps of people who are really good at this sort of thing . . . but not me. I know full well that to have to spring out of bed on three hundred and forty days of the year simply to inform some learned body that once again there was not a single drop of moisture in the bottom of my rain gauge, well, I just wouldn't have it in me, and being the sort of person I am, would be inclined to linger on in bed and spice up the dispiriting readings with a few exciting extra millimetres.

Anyway, Domingo's wheelbarrow and even our flimsy plastic cone were well up to the task of gauging the pathetic amount of rainfall we had in November. December was no better either: short, dry, sunny days; lunch on the terrace. We told friends and family in less favoured parts of the world, where it was gloomy and wet – England, mostly – how glorious our weather was.

Chloé came home from Granada for Christmas. I fetched her from the bus stop in Órgiva. These are some of my favourite moments in life, that small involuntary welling of the heart that must be how dogs feel when they lower their ears and wag their tail. I don't have the same mastery of my ears, and my tail is purely vestigial, but the feeling is there, manifesting itself throughout my thorax whenever I see Chloé or Ana after an absence.

On the journey home, Chloé tried to explain to me the niceties of 'Pragmatics', one of the more unfathomable subjects of her translation and interpretation course, which I happily pretended to understand. This was not going to be a long visit – Chloé intended to head back to the city on Boxing Day – but we knew the score by now and felt happy and pleased to be granted this brief shred of her life. On the night of her arrival, the 23rd of December, to our intense relief and delight, the drought broke and the heavens finally opened. We sat by the fire, the three of us, tucking in to a dish of boar – the last frozen cuts we'd saved for the festivities – and double-shucked *habas*, rejoicing in the waterproofing effect of the green rooves, and listening to the rain as it thundered on the earth of the roof, danced *zapateados* on the skylight, and roared on the corrugated iron of the porch.

This was rain like we had never heard rain before, though, and it made me uneasy. By two in the morning the sound of the roaring of the river that came up from the valley drowned even the infernal thundering of the rain on the roof. I lay wide awake in bed, wondering what we would find in the morning. At four on the morning of Christmas Eve the river sounded as if it were raging from the gorge like the hordes of Beelzebub. The phone rang. Nobody rings you that early in the morning unless there's something really serious going on. I was awake anyway, racked by now with worry as the awful roaring in the valley swelled in a hellish crescendo. It was Domingo.

'Cristóbal,' he said, darkly. 'Can you get me the keys to your car?'

'What do you mean?' I asked, although I had a pretty good idea what he did mean.

'I've been down to the river and it's tearing away the ground beneath the wheels. In half an hour, maybe sooner, you're going to lose your car.'

The car is parked on the far side of the river, on the highest ground in the riverbed, about five metres above the bridge. The keys hang on the back of the kitchen door.

Domingo continued: 'The bridge has gone; you've lost your *acequia*, your water supply, and the track on both sides of the river. The river has completely changed course and is about to take away the fields at the bottom of your farm. It's still growing, and there's no way of knowing what it's going to do. Have you got a set of keys over this side?'

I could tell from the measured way that he was speaking that he was uncharacteristically rattled. I imagined that he had been out all night, rushing around the place fixing leaks and shuffling sheep about, and drenched to the skin, as his waterproof wear is not of the best.

There wasn't an awful lot I could do about any of this: there were no keys on Domingo's side of the river, and there was not a chance in a million of throwing the keys across the river, even if it were not swollen . . . so I went back to bed, where it was warm and dry and the Wife was. Later I lay awake in the pale morning darkness, listening to the hammering of the rain on the flat roof. Had I been a smoker, I would have smoked . . . in fact, this seemed like the perfect moment to take it up. There was a bull here that needed taking by the horns, but I thought it better to wait a bit till daybreak, and perhaps a lull in the rain, and I'd be feeling a lot more equable about things having had another couple of hours supine in bed.

With the first light of the morning I fished out an umbrella, shook the summer's dead scorpions out of my wellingtons and stepped out into the rain. I squelched into a world that, having been hard and dry, had overnight become soft and sodden. The rain was still pouring on down and, although the cataclysmic downpour of the night seemed to have passed, the air was so full of water that it immediately condensed on my glasses. I wiped them with a rag I found in my pocket but it only made them worse, so I took them off and walked myopically and with some trepidation down the track towards the river, the dogs trotting along behind.

We hear the sound of the water all year round: in summer it dwindles to the faintest susurration as the water trickles from pool to pool amongst the rocks, and in winter it's a constant roaring, not unlike the sound of distant traffic on a motorway, the roaring of rubber on a road. It's so constant that you barely notice it. This, though, was entirely different: the valley was awash with noise, the terrible noise of swollen and raging waters. The thunder of boulders crashing into one another punctuated the ceaseless roar of maddened water. Misty clouds moved amongst the mountains, cutting off the tops and creating the illusion of strange hills and crags where there were none. There were slender cascades where there never had been cascades before, tumbling high amongst the Aleppo pines on La Serreta, and, adding to the tumult, the crash and tumble of rockfall after rock-fall, as familiar crags and pinnacles dissolved before my eyes and vanished in the raging grey water.

The dogs moved through this awful scene utterly indifferent to it, sniffing the new smells and wagging their tails. That's the way dogs are: they may or may not be composed largely of love, but they have not the slightest interest in, nor appreciation of, landscape or beauty. They're like teenagers in that respect. As for me, I stood on the corner, my jaw slack, spellbound by the sight of the river in flood. Where were the inoffensive little minnows, I wondered, the tadpoles and frogs, the green lines of tamarisk and oleander that bordered the river where it ran before? They hadn't stood a chance.

The rain lashed on down as I continued towards the lower fields of the farm. I was heavy with water and the mud on my boots. The sheep peered from the stable door as we passed; they weren't going anywhere; they hate to get wet. Finally I caught sight of the Trevélez River, rolling down the valley from the north. There was no way I could even get to where I might be able to see the car: everything had gone. Where there had once been a rich vegetation of trees and bushes, and the road that led to the farm, there was nothing but river. As I stood there, gaping at it all, a whole hedge of brambles, tamarisk and broom came crashing down and whirled away on the flood.

Domingo was right: we had already lost a large part of the lower farm, and the water was still rising and the rain was still sheeting down. The car would be good and gone by now. I felt a bit sad about it, with that curious sense of loss and confusion that you experience when you get to where you thought you left your car in the street . . . and it's not there. And we had lost precious land, too, land that represented years of cultivation and care, of hopes and heady schemes, with olives and oranges and apricots that now would never give fruit. There was nothing to be done, though, so, helplessly and a little numbed by it all, I turned and trudged back up the hill.

Ana and Chloé had woken up by now, and moved into the day, and so after a rather subdued breakfast we decided to climb the hill above the house to get a clearer idea of what was happening. The rain had more or less stopped and given way to a breeze chasing towering clouds across the sky. We climbed, the three of us, to the ridge above the house, where we had a fine view of the whole riverbed, from where the Trevélez River was pouring out into the wider valley, down to the meeting of the waters below the farm; and way up the Cádiar River to where it emerged from its narrow gorge.

I scanned the valley to see if I could see what the river had done with the car. No sign of it; perhaps it had been washed all the way down to the deeper water by the dam. I took my filthy glasses off and wiped them on my shirt. As I did so, Ana nudged me and pointed . . . there was the car, just about visible through my filth-smeared lenses, and almost where I had left it, but on what looked like higher ground a little farther from where the bridge had been. Relief swept over me. Later Domingo told me that he had gone down to the river with his tractor and dragged the car – which was locked, in gear and with its handbrake on – back from the crumbling riverbank. That's neighbourliness . . . and there he had been, racing about in the bucketing rain while I was back in bed, pleasantly tangled with the warmth of the Wife. I made a mental note that some day I would return the favour and do a great act of neighbourliness for Domingo. But then I remembered that his fierce independence and self-reliance made such gestures impossible. Well, I would see what I could do.

The car was still there then, but the change wrought in the valley was almost beyond belief. Before, we had had a valley with earth and flowers and bushes and trees; there had been little Arcadian corners filled with beautiful wild asparagus, and winding paths through groves of towering ailanthus. We had had favourite spots for picking blackberries and figs; mushrooms and puffballs gathered mysteriously in damp shadowy places; and there were abandoned terraces amongst dense hedges of oleander and fallen stone walls, where the deep grass was studded in spring with celandines and margaritas. This was all part of the poor battered botany of the valley, a thousand varieties of flower and bush, bitten off and munched by Domingo's sheep, then masticated, digested and finally excreted in sweet-scented clusters of *cagarutas*, little black berries, that in places literally carpeted the ground, ensuring richness and fertility for the future.

All that was gone. There was nothing to be seen now but a moving mass of water and, where this had subsided a little, a wilderness of grey boulders and gravel. Ana was very subdued. I consider myself to be pretty sensitive about landscape, but I'm not in the same league as my wife, for whom any harm that befalls the plants and trees that surround us is like a personal affront. The destruction we were witnessing was almost more than she could bear. There wasn't really much I could say, either, as we all gazed down upon our ruined valley.

There was no way in or out now; we had lost the road, and the bridge was gone. The *acequia* was completely destroyed, the lifeblood of the farm, which brought water along the hillside from

174

the river. The pipe that had brought our house water from a spring on the far side of the river had been swept away too, and so, ironically, we were without water in the house, for drinking, washing or cooking. The much cherished and nurtured kitchen garden down by the gate was under a metre of silt and gravel, with the river water spreading in a filthy sheet across it. All that work and all that hope, just washed away . . . potatoes, artichokes, greengages.

We stood in silence with our mouths open for a bit, until Chloé drew our attention to some sheep cut off by the water. Down on the corner of the valley, where the two rivers joined, was a gaggle of a dozen or so creatures, wreathed, as is often the way with sheep, in uncertainty and confusion. They were a splinter group separated from Domingo's flock. You could tell; his sheep have no tails. They stood on an island of mud with water swirling around them on all sides; their future didn't look good. They were considering the rising water and trying to come to a mutually acceptable decision, something sheep are not particularly good at.

We hurtled down to the river, hopping and slithering across the sodden ground. It took ten minutes to get there, but when we arrived the place was deserted; there was not a sheep to be seen. It looked as if they had made the wrong decision and left the island on the river side as opposed to the land side, which meant that they would have been swept away. We felt utterly dejected by this, thinking of the poor foolish creatures' panic and terror as the earth gave way and they tumbled headlong into the water. Chloé took it harder than Ana and me, who had farmed sheep for long enough to know that they are certainly the most accident-prone animals on the planet, with the possible exception of lemmings.

For Domingo it would be a blow. He makes his living almost entirely from his sheep, and the loss of a dozen would make a big hole in his meagre earnings.

I think it was fortunate for us that Chloé was home for Christmas that year because without that powerful motive to remain stoical and even attempt some semblance of optimism. Ana and I might have given in to gloom and depression. Christmas spirit was a bit too much of a stretch, but as we trudged back to the house we began to talk about practical matters: how to harvest the rainwater run-off from the roof to tide us over until we could get the pipe from the spring fixed . . . and indeed what we might eat for lunch. Ana retreated for a while to her vegetable patch to assess the depredations of snails and slugs, who might have been brought into being by the wet, and no doubt restore some equilibrium by resting her eyes on what greenery still remained. I had tried to brighten things up with a little homespun philosophy about the give and take of living out in the wild, and how dull our lives would become if things didn't get out of hand from time to time. Chloé rolled her eyes and went off to bring in some dry firewood.

The rest of the day we spent quietly, enjoying, in spite of everything, that peculiar solace that comes from being together and cut off from the rest of the world. The rest of the world could do what it liked; we would content ourselves with each other's company, reading, listening to music, and warming ourselves before a hot fire of almond wood. Then in the evening Chloé and I went down to the stable to shut the sheep in and pick some lemons to make a tart. As we passed the tamarisk wood beside the lemon grove, I saw something woolly and wreathed in uncertainty. It was Domingo's marooned sheep.

'But are you absolutely sure it's the same ones?' Chloé asked hesitantly.

'Well, there's about a dozen of them and two of them are those horrible brown and white things that Domingo seems to like. They must have made the right decision after all.' It was a little thing but it lifted a load from our hearts.

As we shut the gate of the sheep shed, I was struck by a patch of stinging nettles that had been washed clean by the rain, their lush velvety leaves sparkling with tiny drops of moisture. 'I think we'll pick this lot and make a soup out of it, no?' I suggested to Chloé, expecting of course that she would be appalled at the idea of eating stinging nettles; but she wasn't at all.

'I've never had nettle soup,' she said,

matter-of-factly, 'I imagine that they don't sting once you cook them'. She was right. The sting is instantly neutralised the moment you immerse them in boiling water. I sometimes forget that she is no longer a child.

By Christmas Day the rains had stopped. There was still no internet or telephone, as these conveniences seem to go down whenever there's rain or wind. So we settled down to a quiet family meal. Poor Chloé, stranded as she was with the old folks on the hill and thus missing out on all sorts of appealing festivities in Granada, was philosophical, and made a good fist of pretending that she rather preferred to linger on a bit. And the soup was a triumph. You don't normally think of nettle soup as festive fare, but take it from me, if you whizz up your stinging nettles with a little potato for the texture, some garlic and onion, and a red-hot chilli to give it some edge, and you serve it in a dainty bowl with a swirl of soured cream and a handful of small golden croutons, and wash it down with a rich, strong-bodied ruby wine, well, the words will fail you as they're failing me.

Next was lamb. It's always lamb at Christmas. If you keep sheep, you eat lamb. This one glowed in a spicy glaze of pomegranate syrup and chillies, and was stuffed with a whole posy of herbs from the hill. There was *mojo picón* to go with it – parsley, oil and salt ground in the mortar and pestle with a little garlic and green chilli; and crispy roast potatoes; and a lemon tart to finish off.

Good food enjoyed with people you love, I reflected, as I blew out the last of the candles and headed for bed, is a fine antidote to most of the tribulations of existence.

Things, and indeed sheep, being the way they are, a large part of Domingo's flock – of whom the twelve were a mere splinter group – had contrived to be on our side of the river when the rain started, and they were about to start lambing. Just after Christmas seemed an odd time to be lambing, and for this Domingo levelled some of the blame at me. For reasons that need not be explained here, we leave the balls on our ram lambs. When the lambs get big, of course they are apt to cover any fruity ewe that comes within a mile of them, and, rather shamefully, our own flock has been reproducing this way for a number of years now. Domingo's flock, when on our side of the river, is not above wandering over and spending the day grazing on our land. It's no big deal: in a good year there's more than enough grazing for everyone, so I don't say anything about it. But as soon as our ram lambs get a whiff of Domingo's ewes – and there's always one on heat – they're off like big dogs through the scrub, and the inevitable happens. To be fair, I think one of his own rams had got to them, as well, and as they ought not to have been on my land in the first place Domingo was inclined not to be too censorious and I not to feel too racked with guilt. Be that as it may, and whoever the fathers were, the sheep were on the wrong side of the river, and they were lambing. This could have been a disaster: the hillside is teeming with foxes and boar, and they are hungry; well, foxes and boar are always hungry. A fox will wait for a ewe to lamb and then kill and eat the lamb as it emerges. I can think of no more vicious cruelty, but that's the way of the wild. There are eagles too, and, with prey as scarce as it is, an eagle would certainly not be above taking a small lamb. Thus it was a matter of some urgency to get Domingo's sheep back into their stable on their own side of the river.

Five days after the rain, the river had abated sufficiently for Domingo to be able to tie a length of string to a stone and throw it across. We have done this so many times before that we hardly give it any thought. With the string I hauled across a rope, and with the rope I hauled across a steel cable upon which hung a small bag containing a spanner and half a dozen bulldog clips. I selected a suitable tree: the lotus tree, *Celtis australis*, is best for the job with its deep and broad root structure. I sheathed the end of the cable in a plastic hose to protect the bark, passed it twice around the base of the tree, and then crimped it with the bulldog clips and wellied them up good and tight with the spanner.

Meanwhile Domingo connected a winch to his end of the cable on the far side of the river, and when I signalled that my end was good and fixed he whanged the cable up as tight as a string on a fiddle. I have a clip-on pulley and a bosun's chair from the last time we used this contrivance, so I clipped it onto the cable, and, with some trepidation, as the river was still raging beneath me like a thing demented, launched myself into space, pulling myself across the gulf hand over hand. If the contraption had failed, and I had fallen into the river, I wouldn't have lasted thirty seconds, such was the force of the water. But everything held together like I knew it would, and in a couple of minutes Domingo was helping me disentangle myself. I gave him a hug; it was an emotional moment. He winced – he's less demonstrative than I am – but we both recognised the significance of the occasion.

We spent the rest of the day refining the cableway, or 'flying fox' as the device is known, with pulleys and hauling-ropes, and complicated constructions of driftwood and string to raise the cable to the optimum height. And I thanked Destiny, as I have done so many times before, for giving me the extraordinary Domingo as a neighbour and friend.

The next day Domingo secured the services of Manolo to help with the heavy work. Manolo glided blithely across the river (whose menace seemed less today as the water was sparkling in bright morning sunshine), hauled by Domingo and me, and then disappeared up the hill with Domingo and his collie, who had come across on his lap. A couple of hours later they came down with the sheep and shut them in my stable yard. There we trussed them up, tying their legs together with string, and loaded them in groups of six into our farm car. Of course it made a pretty foul mess of the car, but I suppose Domingo considered this just retribution for my part in getting his sheep knocked up, and perhaps there was a certain justice in it.

We drove them to the river and there loaded them three at a time onto a moving platform that Domingo had welded up the previous night. The platform was not a thing of beauty, but as an ad hoc solution to the problem it was nothing short of a masterpiece; it had the necessary strength and was as stable as you could wish for when suspended above a fast-moving river on a single cable. As a small concession to aesthetics he had taken the time to paint it electric blue. Once loaded onto the platform the hapless sheep were winched across the river and heaved off on the other side. Domingo untied their legs and they staggered off looking a bit dazed, until they found something interesting to eat and instantly forgot the whole wretched episode. An endearing quality of sheep is that they harbour no grudges, which, for a sheep farmer, is a great convenience.

Given the complexity of the operation, it took the whole day to get the eighty or so sheep across to Domingo's side of the river, and the work was hard, because the sheep, shortly due to lamb, were enormously heavy with lambs and amniotic fluid and all the other paraphernalia of birth and life. By the end of the day we were all exhausted.

Now that we could communicate with the outside world, Chloé decided that the period of her confinement was up and it was high time she got back to society. We had all wallowed in the unexpected 'quality time' with one another. The fire in the hearth through the long evenings, the candlelight glowing on the white stone walls, conversation, music, home-cooked food and some good wine. I am easily pleased but I imagine that by the end of the week Chloé might have found our home-spun entertainments beginning to wear a little thin. So our daughter put the wheels in motion for her escape to the world over the other side of the river. Domingo had taken the electric-blue platform off, so I fixed up the bo'sun's chair again and in ten minutes we were all three of us across the river, where some friends had arrived with a borrowed mule to take Chloé and her bags up to the road, the track to the river being now impassable for cars.

As we hugged one another goodbye, Bumble, our big white Spanish mastiff, appeared beside us, battered and bedraggled. I could hardly believe that she had launched herself into the raging water and struggled across for no other reason than that we happened briefly to be on the other side. It was little short of a miracle that she had survived. Chloé, delighted by this heroic gesture, smothered her with a big display of affection, while Ana and I tried to disguise our anxiety as to how on earth we'd manage to get the brainless creature home.

Bumble is an enormously strong dog, affectionately known as 'The Lifter', for her endearing habit of thrusting her enormous nose deep into the crotch of unsuspecting visitors and, with a heave of her powerful neck, lifting them off the ground. There are some who find this good-natured demonstration of affection embarrassing; we find it a hoot. But there was little lift left in that poor shaken creature shivering and whimpering beside us.

We looked around, appalled at the possibility that Bumble's little terrier companion, Bao, might have tried the same stunt, because he would immediately have been whipped away by the river. But with great relief we spotted him standing anxiously by the cable on the home bank, watching us with that quizzical tilt of the head with which dogs express bafflement.

So Chloé headed off for Granada, and we applied ourselves to the problem of how we were going to persuade Bumble to cross that river again. There was no way we could carry her across on the bo'sun's chair; we're talking about a sixty-kilo wriggling mass of dog here. Ana and I swung ourselves across and called to Bumble. But she wasn't having any of it: she took a look at the river, decided against it, and headed downstream.

We followed her, calling and calling. She kept stopping and looking at the river as if assessing where might be a safer spot to cross. And there were better places and worse: in places, you would be battered to death in seconds by the water careering over the rocks, and then there were calmer stretches where you just might stand a chance of swimming across before the current hurled you upon the next heap of rocks. She was clearly still exhausted and terrified by her first crossing, and she continued downstream till the river crashed against a cliff and there was no way past, then turned and headed back up, with us still in pursuit on the other bank.

It's about half a kilometre between the cable and the cliff, and as rough and rocky as you could imagine. There was a spot here that looked good – or at any rate less bad. We stopped and concentrated all we could on trying to persuade the pea-brained animal to come across. We shouted into the noise of the water, and we begged and we cajoled and we jumped up and down with all the energy we could muster, for darkness was falling now and not much time remained. Bumble looked at us piteously, tried the river with a toe, and stepped back. We howled. She stepped in again, a little further this time, and was instantly knocked off her feet, disappearing beneath the water as she roiled away down the river only to be smacked hard against a rock. Somehow she righted herself and staggered out of the water on the same side as she had entered.

'Let's try walking away,' suggested Ana. 'She

might pluck up courage if she sees us going home.' So we did, looking back over our shoulders and calling out as we clambered across the rocks. The pitiful creature gazed at us imploringly as we abandoned her, then hurled herself one more time into the water. We raced back to the bank and howled encouragement. Again she vanished beneath the water, hurled downstream by its awful force. We were quiet for a moment . . . and then we saw her again, scrabbling with her claws to haul herself onto a flattish rock in the middle of the river. She slipped and half fell, but her desperation saved her and she heaved herself up and lay limp and exhausted on the rock.

The dog was not more than a dozen metres from us now. We watched her in the dying light, panting in a state of dazed terror, letting her rest a little to recover some strength. And then we yelled together and yelled and yelled at her to throw herself in just one more time and give it all she'd got and she'd be here. She struggled to her feet and moved to the edge of the rock . . . but on the wrong side; she seemed about to head back where she had come from. Ana and I nearly went berserk, screaming our very lungs out. If she got this wrong she would be done for. The river on the far side of the rock was wider and nastier; she had already done the harder bit . . . and now it looked like she was going back. 'BUUMMMBBLE, YOU BRAINLESS BERK! HEEEEERE, OVER HERE!' She sniffed the water, stumbled, and unsteadily shuffled round to look at us, frantic with fear. Ana was almost in tears by now and I was beside myself. And then the wretched dog threw herself into the water towards us. She vanished instantly, dragged under by the current. That awful infinitesimal moment seemed to stretch on and on as we waited to see her head above the water again, but we could see nothing.

We stumbled on downriver over the boulders, peering desperately into the gathering gloom and the tumult for some sight of her, but there was nothing, and we couldn't risk getting any closer to those terrible waters. But still we yelled Bumble's name, as if resisting the thought that we had had our last sight of her.

And then, after twenty or so minutes of this, we stopped. It was dark now. We could barely see the boulders in front of us. We had to accept that she had gone. Another dog down. That's how it is with dogs: they die on you. You have to get over it, and she had had a good innings. I was deeply upset, though. Bumble may have been something of a bimbo but she was affectionate and dependable. Wherever I went, she'd be with me, thumping that enormous tail of hers, making us laugh with her nonsensical notions and habits. Ay, Bumble . . . taken by the river.

I put my arm round Ana's shoulders and we stood there in silence, enveloped by the roaring of the river, as a few more minutes passed. And then, as if by some unspoken agreement, we turned and started to pick our way back towards the house. By the big Eucalyptus tree we stopped and looked back once more towards the river in the dark.

'Well,' I said, 'at least it was quick. I guess it's not a bad way to go. And she never got incontinent, like old dogs do . . .' Ana was silent. I warmed to my theme. 'She's a big dog. You don't want a dog that big being incontinent about the place, do you?'

I had thought I might try and make Ana laugh – although the conceit was not a particularly funny one, and it was hardly a time for levity. A respectable period ought to elapse before one dwelt upon the humorous aspect of a dog's death. And then I laughed. I laughed and laughed. Because there, pale and sodden in the darkness, was the great bedraggled berk of a dog, panting and feebly attempting to wag her tail. We threw ourselves upon her. One hell of a dog, that one.

CHAPTER 12

CRIMES AND PUNISHMENTS

The Flying Fox as a means for getting to and from your home is not for everyone. But I like the surge of adrenalin it adds to a shopping trip into town, and find it oddly reassuring, knowing that we remain in touch with the slower pleasures of rural life. The inordinate amount of time it takes to do such simple tasks as bring in supplies of sheep-feed provides the perfect excuse not to have to tackle the more taxing tasks that hem me in . . . bookwork, the writing of articles, the chasing of deadlines and suchlike. It sounds foolish, but I genuinely enjoyed our time of having no bridge, when everybody and everything had to be winched in.

But our enforced isolation was all too short-lived. There were pressures from all sides. Domingo wanted a bridge to move his sheep easily from one side of the river to the other; the hunters wanted a bridge to come across to our side and massacre the few remaining thrushes, turtledoves and partridges; the Alpujarran authorities wanted a bridge, as it's the only way to cross the river on the GR7 walking path; and, for some unfathomable reason, Ana wanted a bridge, too. And so a new bridge was built.

I have written about the building of bridges before, so I won't burden you with all the details, except to say that I believe this bridge will be the last we build. Domingo was, as ever, the master of the works, and this time, perhaps as a consequence of his new status as a property owner in the valley, he decided to abandon the old Alpujarran tradition of not spending any money on the river. This time he and I shelled out for a couple of substantial RSJs (Rolled Steel Joists), with double-T frames, and some steel sheets to weld across them. We built the new bridge higher above the river than ever before, and raised the joists upon a couple of massive piers of stone, concrete and reinforcing steel. This brutally engineered construct creates an unspeakable clanging and clattering even when the most meagre nocturnal creature creeps timidly across. And when Domingo's whole flock of two or three hundred sheep goes galloping across, the iron thunder rolls away down the river and fills the valley with its horrid cacophony.

This bridge may last for ever but I feel a little ashamed of it. Bridges should be beautiful, like temples; they have their being at points of geographical, mystical and social significance, where the ways meet the water. I have seen the 'wind and rain bridges' of Guangxi in China, painstakingly constructed from wood, without the use of a single steel nail; I've seen Pont Neuf in

Paris, and the Rialto in Venice, to say nothing of hundreds of more unassuming beauties that just get on uncomplainingly with the noble business of transporting people and goods across the water. There's nothing noble about our bridge, though, with its artless assemblage of junk.

It took us two days to build the bridge, or rather, for me to assist Domingo in its construction. For, despite having been involved in the building of countless bridges over the past twenty years, I don't seem to have moved one rung up the ladder of seniority and am always given the most menial of tasks, the erk's work.

In this case it was the gathering and humping of heaps of enormous rocks for infill and the construction of the piers. As the work progressed, the supply of acceptable and useful stones became ever scarcer, ever further up the river from the site of the works, and so each stagger and stumble along the rocky water's edge, hugging a rock as big as a small pig, became more of an agony. We are all of us older now than when we built earlier bridges, and the youthful horseplay and capering that lightened our load in those days has given way to a generalised grumbling and groaning and clutching of aching backs and bones. Still, I wouldn't want it any other way. When the day comes that we can no longer throw a bridge across the river, that'll be the day to throw in the towel and move to suburbia.

*　　*　　*

It wasn't a big job to fix up a bridge, but the *acequia* was a very different matter. The river had swept the whole irrigation channel away, leaving only the steep rock upon which, by some long-forgotten wizardry, it had been built. Looking at where its course had been, I could only marvel at how the ancients had been able to achieve it. The rock was hard granite and smooth like the side of a whale. Somehow, in the way that swallows will build a nest on a vertical wall with spittle and mud, my farming predecessors had managed to drill holes with hammers and chisels, drive wooden pegs in and run beams along the pegs. On top of the beams they had started with tiny stones and earth, and little by little incorporated greater stones until finally they had a channel which they lined with clay or launa to waterproof it. Every winter the swelling of the river would bring down silt, and, as this was cleared out and carefully piled upon the fragile banks, plants began to grow, and little by little their root systems bound the banks and walls together.

By the time we came along, maybe a thousand years after this process was started, there were poplar trees with the girth of a wine barrel growing all along the *acequia*. Its precarious origins had vanished beneath a solid mass of earth and vegetation.

To rebuild the wrecked *acequia* in such manner would have been impossible without a team of skilled labourers and spending huge sums of money. But to lose it felt like a dereliction of duty. The *acequia* is a monument of the same vintage as the

Alhambra. It may lack something of the Alhambra's architectural distinction, but for a small farm it was pretty good, and I would be the first in a very long line of farmers to abandon it. I felt worse still when I thought of all the hundreds of hours that Manolo and I and others had spent maintaining the irrigation channel. I had sweated buckets and nearly broken my back cleaning that *acequia*, and often walked along it, too, just for the sheer pleasure. As well as being a thing of singular beauty, with its own ecosystem of plants and tiny creatures, the *acequia* was the very lifeblood of the farm.

By April the moisture from the copious winter rains was dwindling as the spring sunshine warmed the earth. If the trees and crops on the terraces were to survive, we would soon have to find a way of watering. Manolo, who is good at this sort of thing, reckoned that we could cut a new *acequia*, but much lower than the old one, which of course would have the disadvantage that it wouldn't take water to the higher parts of the farm. He had walked the heap of boulders and riverine rubble that now formed the bank of the river, and established where the channel could join it.

When I saw the spot, though, I realised that it would be quite impossible: it would take a team of men six months to move all the boulders and dig the channel. 'It can't be done, Manolo; there's no way you and I can shift that lot. We'd need a machine, and I really can't see how a machine would be able to get anywhere near the river here.'

It looked horribly like the end of the line for my belovèd El Valero, at least as a functioning farm. But Manolo was not to be deterred. 'Pepe Pilili's in the valley,' he said. 'I saw him as I came in this morning; he's fixing up the track. Why don't you go over and see him. He'll do the job for us.'

So I crossed the valley to where Pepe was working, and he said he'd come that afternoon to have a look.

'God, the river's made a mess of this valley,' he announced, as he scrambled up from the bridge.

'I know that, Pepe. I don't need to hear that again. Just tell me if you could get your machine across the river and if you could cut me a new *acequia* here.'

We all walked along the bank towards the gorge, Pepe limping a little.

'No trouble. I'll be over tomorrow afternoon and we'll see what we can do.'

Pepe Pilili used to be cocky and completely incompetent – he had tried and failed to build a road for us when we first moved to El Valero. But after many years of messing about in machines, years which he reckons have wrecked his health, for he hobbles like a crone, he is now cocky, bold and skilled.

'So,' I reported to Manolo. 'Pepe will get it all sorted out for us.'

'As I told you,' said Manolo with a broad grin. 'The only problem now is the permission. You need a permit from the Confederación Hidrográfica to work in the river.'

'Well, I can hardly get a permit before tomorrow, can I? And when was the last time you saw an inspector from the Confederación Hidrográfica? I've been here for more than twenty years and I've never seen one.'

Manolo laughed. 'You're right: I've never seen one either. But if one were to come, he'd have your balls. You know how it is with the authorities.'

In fact, it was three days before Pepe battled his way through the river to our farm – still no time for a permit – and no mean feat of JCB manoeuvring, as there was still a whole lot of water raging on down.

Pepe began to work his way along the bank, digging and levelling as he went. It was a truly amazing sight. A JCB with a good operator can do just about anything, from shouldering aside colossal rocks to the most delicate sort of bottoming up. I watched for a couple of hours, and reckoned it a couple of hours well spent; there's great pleasure in watching well-handled machinery. Then, leaving Manolo as banksman – which in effect meant that he got to lean on his mattock and watch the machine all day long – I walked back up to the house to busy myself with the sort of things you do in a house.

For a few hours I peered at my laptop screen, opening and closing files and deleting the odd email, but my heart was not in it; I wanted to be down by the river where the action was, watching the machine work. So, late in the morning, I headed back down. On the way I met Manolo, who was striding up the track with a huge grin on his face.

'*Hola*, Manolo,' I said. '*¿Qué pasa?* How's it coming along?'

'Bad,' he said. 'You're in trouble. Big, big trouble. The river inspectors are here. And they don't like what's going on, not one little bit. They are very, very angry, and they've stopped Pepe working and they want to see you.' His grin threatened to part the hemispheres of his head.

Together we turned and strode down to face the music, although it wasn't really Manolo's music. It was me who would be carrying the can. With each step I could feel myself winding up into a tighter and tighter knot of defensive fury. 'How dare these bastards come and stop me trying to save my farm,' I growled darkly to myself. 'I'm not going to take this lying down . . . not bloody likely. I've got my rights. I'll hit them with some plain truths.' By the time I got to where Pepe's JCB was standing idle. I'd dispensed with the plain truths idea and was ready for rage.

Two mild-mannered youths, about Chloé's age, stepped forward to greet me, each with a sympathetic grin. The wind spilled from my sails, and we all shook hands and introduced ourselves.

'So what's going on down here?' one of them asked. 'Have you got permission from the Confederación Hidrográfica to do this?'

'I'm afraid not. The job had to be done, and

there happened to be the machine in the valley, so we just got on with it.'

'You are aware', the gentle youth apologised, 'that you need permission to undertake any work in the riverbed?'

'Of course – and I'm sorry that I haven't got permission. But it was a matter of getting things done. As you can see, the river has destroyed everything here and I'm just doing what I can to get some water to my farm.'

'*Claro* – we can see that – and we really do understand that there are extenuating circumstances. To tell you the truth, I don't blame you at all. But I'm afraid that because we've seen what you're up to here, we have to put in a report.'

'I suppose so,' I said miserably. 'Can we finish the job, though?'

'Well, that's up to you. I can't give you permission. But what I suggest is that, to make things easier, you might want to go and see our boss in Granada, explain the situation.' I wrote the boss's details on a piece of paper resting on the bonnet of their car. We talked a little more of the river and the flood and the unspeakable things that people did in the river without permission, and then they drove away.

'What are we going to do then, Cristóbal?' asked Pepe.

'Finish the job off. They've gone now. *Ya que estamos en el baile, bailemos.*' Which translates, rather lamely, as 'Now we're at the dance, let's dance'. It is not perhaps as good an expression as being hung for a sheep as a goat (which of course would be particularly apt in these parts), but it's how the Spanish put it. And they like this sort of thing. A saying is a *refrán* in Spanish, and cultured speakers are described, approvingly, as *muy refraneros*.

Not long afterwards I took the bull by the horns – *cogí el toro por los cuernos* (as the *refrán* has it) – and set off to see the Hidrográfica boss in Granada. I knew that the fines imposed by the river authority for unauthorised messing with the river could be ruinous. And rightly so, for the water of the rivers is a public resource that should belong to everybody, and yet there are no end of villains, both private and corporate, who are engaged in siphoning off more than their fair share. It's hardly unreasonable to expect to have to get authorisation for any use of the public resource. However, I did hear later that a friend whose *acequia* had similarly been damaged in the flood, had applied for permission and that permission did not come through for eighteen months. Of course, all the trees that he needed to water were dead by then. So I felt a certain justification in pitching in and getting on with the job.

Nonetheless, every day I was regaled by new horror stories of farmers ruined by colossal fines for the most minimal infraction of the rules. For some time Hidrográfica fines were Manolo's sole topic of conversation, which rather ruined the pleasure of our hour of *manualidades*. Schadenfreude, as I think I have said somewhere before, is a common trait in the Alpujarra, a good-natured delight, even hilarity, when things go desperately wrong for the neighbours. That's not to say that they won't pitch in and help out with great generosity and enthusiasm to make whatever it was that went wrong go right again.

If you're feeling remotely in need of an uplifting experience, the austere seat of the River Authority in Granada would be the wrong place to look for it. The offices are dark and slightly grubby, with not the least attempt to create a pleasing environment for work or visitors, no decorations except for a few torn posters announcing union meetings and the odd exhortation not to waste water. I felt a little nervous, in the way I tend to feel when entering a hostile environment, because, let's face it, public administrative bodies are pretty hostile environments, and the plywood-partitioned rooms and frosted glass of the tenth floor did nothing to allay that feeling.

I had an appointment for the start of business at 8.30am, but when I arrived – on the dot – there were some men already in there. I kicked my heels in the corridor, trying to feign interest in boxes of papers and photocopiers. I couldn't sit down and read a book, firstly because I was too agitated to concentrate and, secondly, there wasn't a chair . . . and besides, I hadn't brought a book.

After a while the men left and I walked into the office, about as depressing as an office can be, and with an incumbent to match. The Confederación Hidrográfica official was short, I think, although it was hard to tell, as he was sitting behind a desk and seemed reluctant to rise and greet me. He had a beard and was dressed in a brown shirt and tie.

The official barely registered my entrance and it transpired that he didn't know anything about my case and nor was he much interested by it. After listening a little, while signing papers in a file in front of him, he suggested dismissively that I go to the floor below and talk to the secretaries about applying for permission retrospectively. I was a little surprised by his brusqueness, but what did I expect? I was the felon, after all, and he was a *funcionario*, a civil servant, one of a section of society well known in Spain for their dismissive attitude to the public.

Things were different on the floor below. There was a lot more femininity, for a start, with four women hovering around what seemed to be an information desk. One of them smiled and asked how she could help me. I told her my sorry tale while the rest stopped what they were doing to listen. The first woman, Consuelo her name was, gazed at me intently until I had finished, at which point she piped up with: 'You're the one who wrote that book, aren't you?'

'Yes,' I replied a little surprised.

'I liked the book,' she said, smiling even more warmly. 'So, if there's ever anything I can do to help, then I'd be happy to do it.' And so saying, she ushered me to an office at the end of the passage and introduced me, with all the pride and care you might reserve for a favourite brother, to the older woman behind the desk. 'She'll tell you the best way to present your case,' I was reassured.

And indeed she did. I went home with instructions to prepare, in triplicate, a sketch of the site, a photo of the site before and after the work was carried out, a description of the site, a description of the work to be carried out, a sketch of the farm, a sketch of the river, an account of why I had failed to follow the correct procedures, a photocopy of the deeds of the farm, a photocopy of my identity document, a photograph of me, a document sworn in front of a public notary to say that I was who I said I was, and another to say that the photo resembled the person it purported to be, which was me . . . There was something else, too, but I forgot what it was.

I drove home over the hills, eager to get going, and a couple of days later I sent the whole shebang in a big, buff certified envelope to the Confederación Hidrográfica, and sat back to await results.

Now of course one doesn't expect a quick reply from such a body and, as the weeks fled by, I might almost have forgotten all about the whole episode, were it not for Manolo reviving the subject in ever more spectacularly gloomy terms during *Manualidades*.

'A man in Tablones had to sell his car and all his goats to pay the fine – and that was just for shifting a couple of rocks in the river. Juan Barquero knows a man who had to sell his farm and move away to another province . . . You might even have to go to prison,' he added happily, while I hammered yet another almond into smithereens.

About six weeks later I found stuffed in my post office box a certified letter from the river authority. It told me that I had failed to append one of the required documents in appropriate form, and would I do the whole thing again and do it properly this time. The document conveying to me this information ran to five pages of incomprehensible codswallop. I scanned it in a perfunctory manner. At the end it said something about six months' grace. I took this to mean that I didn't have to lift another finger until the expiry of the six months, and having duly noted five months and twenty-nine days thence in my diary, forgot all about it. Well, 'forgot all about it' may be not entirely appropriate, given that twice a week during *Manualidades* I was reminded in the most lurid terms of the potential nightmare ramifications of my misdeed. Domingo and Juan Barquero had taken up this refrain, too, and so every time I bumped into one or other of them I would be regaled with the same litany.

So on the twenty-ninth day of the fifth month after that initial notification, I fished out the document from what is affectionately known by my women as my 'toy box'. Having not seen it for a bit, I scanned the document with a little more care and comprehension. Lord knows where I had got the 'six months' from. It said that I had but ten days from receipt of the registered letter to get the whole business in order . . . thus I was five months and nineteen days too late. Manolo and Domingo and Juan would be ecstatic. The shit was really going to hit the fan now.

I was seized with anguish about this, for, according to my friends and informants, this default would probably multiply by ten the already ruinous ramifications of my original crime. Failing to read the document correctly was no defence, as it is, apparently, the duty of the citizen to be properly informed. The whole thing made me feel very uneasy and nervous, and each passing week only added to my agitation about the outcome of my case.

And then I sat back and thought about it: more than six months had passed since I had failed to provide the authority with the correctly and duly filled-in forms . . . Perhaps they had forgotten.

'No, they never forget,' Manolo kindly assured me as he sliced off a thick lump of *chorizo* to go with his beer. 'Sometimes they let it go on for years, and all the time the fine is increasing and you don't even know. It's a bad business, a bad business.' And he shook his head in a feeble attempt at fellow feeling.

Lost in thought I attacked a few more *habas*. 'I tell you what, Manolo: I'm just going to let it slide, forget the whole cussed issue. Sod 'em, I did my best, and if that's not good enough for them, well . . . well . . .'

'Well what?'

'Well . . . we'll just see what happens.' And at that I scooped the *habas* and their outer shells into the same bucket, thus wasting a good half hour's work.

Despite my bravado, I was quite seriously worried. Stressed, in fact. As the worry grew, I started to come out in boils, and all manner of unpleasant ailments began to assail my person. This thing was in me and doing me harm.

Then one day notification of a registered letter arrived in my post office box from Medio Ambiente – the Environment Department. I was on my way out, going away for a week, so I decided not to accept the letter then; I would pick it up when I came back. Of course, by the time I did come back, the post office, in their inimitable way, had returned the letter to the sender. The direst forebodings began to haunt me. I didn't need corroboration from my neighbours to know that I had gone too far this time. The administration would be really riled up and out to get me for all I had got. I found it hard to get to sleep at night.

They kept me in this awful suspense for another month, and then there it was, a pink slip back in the post office box. I collected the letter from the desk, signed for it, and went to sit down in a bar so that I would not fall over when I discovered the terrible truth. I ordered a coffee and looked at the envelope for a bit, then tore into it. '*LEVE*' was the first word I saw, because it was in capitals. *Leve* means 'light' . . . it seemed that my misdemeanour was being considered by the administration as 'light', i.e. not serious. I read on. The denouement was on the last of five pages: if within thirty days you have not appealed against our decision, you must pay a fine of ninety euros. Ninety euros! That was probably about a fifth of what the original permission would have cost me, had I applied for it.

This was as good a piece of news as the news that somebody wants ninety euros off you can be. I resolved to pay the fine without further ado, and accordingly scanned the rest of the letter to see how one went about paying it. It seemed that I would need a form called *Modelo 047*. I went back to the post office, because sometimes you can pay these things through that august institution, but no, they hadn't the first idea what a *Modelo 047* was, or how to go about paying the fine.

'Try the bank,' they suggested.

Our local bank in Órgiva moves with the times. Given that a fair proportion of their clientele is English-speaking, they have decided to get in on the act. The first manifestation of this forward-looking policy was a big poster in the bank and a set of fliers in a heap on the counter. These advertised 'On-Linen Banking', and underneath the announcement of this unusual service, the baldly mendacious statement, 'We Speak English'. They don't speak English. Apart from the very charming Augustín, who can greet you with a garbled and almost unrecognisable 'goomorrnin', and might on occasions be persuaded to count from one to ten, nobody has a word of anything but Spanish. So if you go in there hoping to do your banking – on linen or anything else – in English, you're on a hiding to nothing.

That's OK. They're nice people and do what they can to run a halfway decent bank. As a consequence of once having had a bestselling book, we are treated in the bank as high rollers, and Augustín in particular is always at pains to ensure that our every whim is catered for. He seems to be in a constant state of agitation about the parlous state of our accounts, the utter fiscal chaos that reigns amongst them, the complete disregard for sensible banking practice. Now, the rates of interest paid to its customers by our bank are exiguous to say the least; you'd make more money if you lent it to a goat. But even so, our cavalier attitude is a source of constant distress to Augustín, and he is always on the lookout for one or other of us to 'have a talk about it'.

He got hold of Ana a few months ago; she was in the bank and unable to slither away quickly enough.

'Ana,' said Augustín, 'I think that between us we could make a better job of organising your financial situation.'

'*Claro*, Augustín,' she said, trying to sidle off.

'We need to maximise the growth potential of

your deposits,' he continued. 'You understand what I'm saying?'

Ana did understand what he was saying, but he thought he would illustrate the point with metaphor anyway.

'Just think of the bank as a chestnut tree, and your accounts are like the chestnuts, or a cherry tree if you like, and cherries. Then think of your-selves as squirrels, or badgers perhaps . . .'

On and on went the convoluted wildlife talk, sporadically illustrated with graphs and tables that bore no resemblance whatever to badgers and squirrels. Ana could make neither head nor tail of what he was on about, and was only able to get away by promising to send me in to discuss matters.

Thus betrayed by my own wife, I was unable to go anywhere near the bank for a long time. You'll think us foolish perhaps, but sexing up the perfor-mance of our bank affairs would mean the difference between, say, a taxable interest of ten euros forty-seven cents per annum, and one of seventeen euros fifty-three. And a long session with Augustín droning on about cherries and chestnuts and farmers and their lemon trees, over a matter of seven euros and six cents – well, it hardly seemed worth the candle.

But to cut to the chase: having drawn a blank with the *Modelo 047* at the post office, where they hadn't a clue about it, and in the town hall, where Mari-Ángeles the lady mayor was out having coffee, I decided to try the bank, in the hope that Augustín might not be waiting for me.

To check that he wasn't there I peered through the double-doored security airlock (a curious invention that means you can't get in while another person is trying to come out). It was rather dark in there. There was a figure waiting for the electronic permission to burst out into the rarefied atmosphere of the high street, with its smell of coffee, roasting chicken and patchouli oil. And then, bang! – the door flew open – and there like some sort of fairy godmother stood Augustín. He looked at me censoriously.

'Goomorrnin Cristóbal,' he said.

'Ah, Augustín . . . er, I was just going into the bank,' I explained, purposefully.

'What for, Cristóbal? Can I be of help?'

'Um, no, I don't want to molest you during your coffee break.'

'No, let me see. What is it?'

'Oh, it's a fine that I have to pay to Medio Ambiente. It's not a lot of money but I can't work out how to go about paying it and nobody seems able to help me. I need, apparently, to get hold of a *Modelo 047.*'

'*047?*' said Augustín with a chuckle. 'That's easy: you just download it from the Internet, fill it in. All they want is your name and address and the amount of money to be paid and that's it, *pan comido.*'

'Simple as that?'

'Simple as that. Here, give it to me and I'll do it after my coffee; it'll only take a minute.'

'A thousand thanks, Augustín, that's so kind of

you,' and I was almost on the verge of adding, 'maybe we could sit down for a bit and see if we can't make some sense of our bank accounts', but some blessed angel drew me back from the brink. So I went off into the town to deal with a few other pressing matters.

When I passed the bank again – Órgiva is not such a big town that you can go anywhere without repeatedly passing the bank – there were no customers, so I decided to nip in and check that the transaction had gone through.

'Ah, Cristóbal,' said Augustín. 'I haven't done it yet; I got busy. We'll do it right now.' And he moused about with the computer on his desk. He scrolled down, clicked a bit, and moused some more . . . a bit more fast-mousing and a couple of clicks. He frowned, reached for the form I had given him, scanned it a bit, frowned some more and returned to mousing.

I leaned on the counter, took my glasses off in case I would have to sign something, then put them on again when it became manifestly apparent that I wouldn't be signing anything soon.

'*047*,' said Augustín. 'Hmm. There's an *046* and an *048*, but I can't find the *047*. It doesn't seem to be here.'

He frowned some more and flipped through the five pages of the document.

'I know what we'll do,' he said brightly. 'We'll ring them. There's a number here.'

He dialled a number. The phone rang four or

five times, then came a long, speedily jabbered formula, ending in something like 'How may I help you?'

'It's Augustín from the bank in Órgiva . . .' At this, he was cut off, and I heard synthesised muzak. Augustín raised his eyebrows and grinned at me conspiratorially. I shifted from one leg to the other. The muzak went on. It was, as far as I could gather, a cod 'Für Elise', played on an electronic glockenspiel. After about five minutes, during which Augustín continued mousing and clicking in a small way, the muzak stopped. There was silence.

'Speak to me,' said Augustín. '*Dígame.*'

But nobody did; there was nobody there.

He frowned again and leafed through the papers, then dialled another number. I could hear the ringing, and then another jabbered formula.

'It's Augustín here, from the bank in Órgiva, and I've got a customer who wants to pay a . . .'

'You'll be needing an *047*, then,' said the telephone voice.

'Yes, but . . .'

'Wait, I'm going to give you another number to ring.'

Augustín jotted down the number and, with a sigh, dialled it. He gave me a look of mock despair, and grinned, but wanly, then dialled the next number he had written on my form. After the inevitable jabbered reply he started doodling as more muzak – a jaunty Casio-generated flamenco number this time – played. I found myself wondering what Kafka would have made of telephone muzak.

'Good day. It's Augustín here from Órgiva and I want to pay a fine to the department of the environment . . .'

'It'll be a *Modelo 047* you want. . .'

'Yes, but I don't seem to be able to download it. . .'

'That's because you can't download the *047*; only the *046* . . .'

'What do I do, then?'

There was a silence, during which Augustín fiddled with his biro.

'I tell you what: I'll give you another number to ring; this is not really my department, you see . . .'

I smiled gratefully at Augustín. I could see that his patience was soon going to run out, but I wanted to keep him hanging in there till we got some sort of a result. I shook my head in friendly collusion, tipped my hat back on my head, shifted from one leg to the other, leaned in a different direction on the counter and cleared my throat in an amiable way.

Augustín dialled the new number and avoided looking directly at me while he awaited results. Soon a person came on the line who seemed to know what we were talking about, and to have a sound grasp of administrative procedure. '. . . so I think you ought perhaps to get in touch with Madrid,' I heard him say.

I can hardly expect you to believe me when I

say that Augustín made no less than nine telephone calls in search of information on how to pay my fine, and in the end threw in the towel. 'I'm so sorry, Cristóbal,' he said, 'but it's beaten me. I cannot see the way through to solve this problem. Forgive me, but you're on your own.'

I was starting, by this time, to think in an urgent way about some lunch, so I was quite relieved when Augustín finally admitted defeat. I went home for lunch: nettle soup again. And as I sat at my soup I flipped my way through the letter again. It was pretty unfathomable stuff, but all in all I figured that we had been going about it in the wrong way. I reckoned that what I ought to do was to sign the letter, in order to give the impression that I was in agreement with what it said – which broadly speaking I was – and then send the signed letter back to Medio Ambiente. Upon receipt of the aforementioned letter, they might in the fullness of time see fit to send me a copy of the undownloadable (I despise that word) *Modelo 047*. Thereafter I could hand over their, or rather my, ninety euros and rest easy once more.

This I did, and at the moment of writing – two years, and counting, after consigning the letter (registered) to the post, I'm still waiting for a reply.

CHAPTER 13

AN AUTHOR TOUR (WITH SHEEP)

I was on a rare shopping trip to town, buying a couple of concrete pipes that I could no longer do without . . . and some crème fraîche to accompany a crop of late summer raspberries. I stopped to fill up with diesel.

'Eenglish!' A hoarse croak. I looked around. 'Eenglish!' once more. There's only one person who calls me 'Eenglish', and that's José Guerrero, my old sheep-shearing partner. 'Eenglish' is the only word of English he knows.

It was, indeed, he. I grinned with pleasure and strolled over to where he stood, leaning against the back of his van. I gave him an affectionate hug, not an easy thing to do because he's a lot taller than me and I have to reach up on tiptoe, which makes me feel uncomfortably feminine. Perhaps I should stop the hugging and just shake his great bony frying-pan-sized hand, but hell, I love the guy, for all his roguish badness, and we have over the years been through thick and thin together. And I had not seen him in a long time.

'Hey, Guerrero. So how are you doing?'

He coughed in what I thought was an alarming way.

'*Estoy hecho un hacha* (I'm made like an axe),' he growled. He is a singularly artistic user of the Spanish language, which is one of the reasons I appreciate his company.

'Looks like it's your lucky day, bumping into me in town,' he announced. 'Look what I've got for you here.'

He led me to the back of the van and opened the door. A stink of sheep burst from the over-heated boot. I staggered a little, theatrically, for actually there is nothing I like more than the sweet smell of wool and sheep shit; it weaves an olfactory spell that carries me far away and long ago.

'BUAUUGGHH . . . don't you know how to exercise the most basic elements of hygiene, Guerrero?'

'You're getting soft,' he said. 'That's the smell of life itself.' And he kissed his fingertips ecstatically.

'So what have you got for me, then?' I was curious. He lit a cigarette and blew a cloud of smoke into the back of the van, and looked at me expectantly, tapping his foot. I peered into the dark interior, stuffed with shearing machines, boxes of the arcane paraphernalia of sheep-shearing and mephitic piles of shearing clothes. There were a couple of crates of wine in there, too.

'One of those is for you – twelve bottles of the best Ribera del Duero you've ever tasted.'

I looked at my old friend in amazement. I mean, I have done him the odd favour in the past, but if there was a debt at all – and I didn't recall one – then it would be worth a couple of drinks at the most.

'No, they're not from me,' he explained. 'They're a present for you from some friends of mine who run a little hotel up Aranda way on the River Duero. These people are your greatest fans; they're just crazy about your books. I gave them the one with the parrot on the cover – you know, the one with me in it – and they just loved it.'

Now, there is nothing Ana and I like more than a good Ribera del Duero, and you don't look a gift horse in the mouth, so before Guerrero could change his mind I humped the crate into my car, which was, rather uncivically, still parked by the pump at the petrol station. Paco, whose petrol station it is, was watching this operation with interest. He walked over and stood beside José.

'We're having a party. We're going to eat some goat, drink a little wine . . . You want to come along?'

'When?' I asked warily.

'Right now.'

'I can't. I've got to get home.'

'Why?'

I paused at this. It was unlikely they'd share my sense of urgency about the crème fraîche. 'Because . . . because my wife is expecting me,' I replied.

'You're not your own man, Eenglish,' said Guerrero.

'José is right,' echoed Paco. 'You're soft.'

If the truth be told, I didn't much fancy the goat option; we'd have to kill the poor animal for a start, and drink vast quantities of wine, most of it from the crate I'd just been given, while waiting for the goat to char slowly. And, as for the conversation . . . well, it would be man-talk – and man-talk wears thin pretty quickly. So, undoubtedly soft, and my own man or not, I stuck to my guns and sailed out of the garage, setting course for the hills and home.

On the way I considered the evening ahead, sitting out in the fading light on the terrace with the Wife, eating fresh raspberries from the garden with a dollop of crème fraîche and a nice bottle of Ribera to finish it off. It seemed like a wise choice to me.

'Eh, Eenglish!' Guerrero again, on the phone this time, a month or so later. 'We're going to the north next week, you and me. We're going to eat the most fantastic food and drink, a whole lot of wine and we're going to see sheep, beautiful sheep like you've never seen sheep before . . . imagine.'

I could well imagine. This wouldn't be the first such adventure we had embarked upon. They tended not to turn out well. 'Ah, maybe you are,' I countered, 'but I'm not. I've got too much to be doing at home.'

'You have to come; we're going to meet some really interesting people like that Jesús and Eugenia in Aranda, you know, the ones who are so mad about your books, and there'll be *chicas* too, slinky sexy *chicas* like you never dreamed of . . . and, besides, I need your car. For the wine,' he explained. 'We're going to want to stock up in Aranda and all those crates are not going to fit in my car . . . are they?'

It was this that got me thinking the trip might not be such a bad idea. Ana and I had already got through those bottles from Aranda, and we loved them. It was a long time since we had drunk anything so good – rich and smooth with just an infinitesimal effervescence – and this from a small-scale producer, and organic to boot. It would be a shame to miss an opportunity to get to know the producers of this nectar.

And so, having squared things with the Wife, I signed up for the expedition, and threw in the car too . . . and a load of my books in Spanish that, for some unaccountable reason, Guerrero had thought might be useful along the way. 'You never can tell when you might need one,' he said, a little mysteriously.

The hounds, who habitually bay at my heels for things that ought to have been done and yet are left undone, I fobbed off with a pack of lies, and, on an unusually cold morning in November, shivering in the pre-dawn mists, we set off.

José insisted on driving. 'You drive like an old woman,' he said. 'If you drive, we're never going to get there.'

Perhaps I should have protested this slight to the automotive side of my manliness; after all, I consider myself quite sharp and speedy behind the wheel, but in fact I was rather pleased with the idea of being able to laze a bit and enjoy the scenery. And what scenery it was: a little nausea-inducing at first, as Guerrero hurled us round the tight curves of the narrow road between Órgiva and Lanjarón. I held gingerly on to my guts and marvelled at the spectacular view of the sea far below and, unless I was much mistaken, the faintest glimpse of the first snow on the Rif in Morocco. Directly below us were hillsides of olive and almond, dropping all the way down to the Guadalfeo, the river that drains the Western Alpujarra. Then, in no time at all, we were out of the mountains, rocketing across the white bridge over the Tablate gorge, and racing down the sliproad onto the motorway.

I settled back to enjoy the long haul up the hill through the Valle de Lecrín, lush and bright at this time of year with ripening oranges and lemons. Guerrero lit what must have been his fifth cigarette of the journey, filling with smoke the only small pocket of clear air that remained in the car. I opened the window. Out went the smoke; in came a bone-chilling icy gale.

'SHUT THE WINDOW, MAN! We'll freeze to death.'

'Not bloody likely; I need some air to breathe.'

I don't object to cigarette smoke, particularly if

it comes from roll-ups or good black tobacco, but José smoked Marlboro and it filled the car with the filthiest, most acrid miasma. I couldn't take it. I opened all the other windows, too. Guerrero glared at me and growled something I didn't catch, hugging his jacket around his bony frame.

On top of the dashboard, cunningly draped with an old red shirt, he had set up his speed trap warning device, which was plugged into the cigarette lighter. 'This little machine is going to save us a whole lot of money in traffic fines,' he announced. 'I wouldn't go anywhere without it.'

Almost as he spoke, and we had barely been on the motorway for five minutes, the thing started to screech like a demented cricket, gaining in intensity and frequency as we approached the danger. He eased off the gas and we passed by the radar trap at a more equable sort of a speed than the 150 at which we had been travelling.

'Now, your job is to keep an eye out for the *cabrones* of *Tráfico*, and if they get anywhere near us you disconnect the box and poke it all down in the footwell. If they catch us with this, we're stuffed; it's four hundred euros straight down the line and they'll break your balls for it. They don't like 'em.' But the danger passed; the cricket went back to sleep; the fifth cigarette was finished; I closed the windows; Guerrero hit the gas again; and the poor old car resumed its headlong flight towards Granada.

Any notions I might have entertained about a

relaxed sightseeing trip enlivened by bouts of pleasant conversation, shot out of the window along with the smoke. My heart hit my boots as Guerrero got his phone out, peered down at it and, with his elbow propping the steering wheel in position, proceeded to jab out a text message.

The received wisdom is that stress is bad for you. I am not altogether convinced, and believe that a certain level of stress may be beneficial, in that it puts backbone into the flaccid man. But the level of stress that was building in the car was like nothing I have ever experienced; it was moving off the edge of the scale. Imagine if you will:

José is driving the car – a car conceived to operate smoothly at around 120 kilometres per hour – at somewhere between 150 and 160. At 140, the poor old thing seems to go through a barrier of violent juddering that frightens the life out of you. By 147, you've come through on the other side, but the gears are whining, the engine screaming, there's air roaring through the gaps in the closed windows and there is an almost tangible sense of instability. A constant rain of insects immolate themselves, splattering against the windscreen, and the car rocks and rolls like a stagecoach. And you know only too well that to get back to the normal range of speeds you have to pass again through that terrifying band of violent vibration.

On top of all this, José had decided that we needed some exciting music to buck us up and speed us on our way. He looked disdainfully through my selection of cassettes; nothing in it was nasty and noisy enough, though. Well, you get like that with the passing of the years. 'This is what we'll have,' he announced, triumphantly fishing a tape from his pocket. 'Jorge Troghouwahb.'

'And who the in the name of hell is Jorge Troghouwad?' I asked incredulously.

'Jorge Troghouwad is a genius. Hell, I can't speak your language, read the cover!'

I looked at the cover. 'George Thorogood and the Destroyers – Bad to the Bone,' it said.

He slipped the cassette into the deck and turned the volume up, lit another cigarette – whereupon I reopened all the windows – and embarked upon an outrageous account of an amorous evening he had spent in the summer, with a bespectacled librarian from Santa Fe. The phone and the cigarettes occupied only one of his hands, but in order to get across the full salaciousness of his tale, he took, to my extreme alarm, both hands off the wheel. It was a good story but I was glad when it was over.

Coming down over the next pass, the cricket began to get agitated again. José braked hard; the car slewed a little and then shook like a dog in a river as the speed dropped through the critical band. A blessed moment of less terrifying speed. I was growing to look forward to the respite given me by the screeching of the cricket.

The phone rang. José checked the screen, and raised it to his ear. '*Dime primo. ¿Qué te pasa?*' (Tell me, cousin, what's happening? – where 'cousin' is a gipsy form of greeting, very friendly.) He listened carefully, or as carefully as the deafening music and the screaming of the engine and the howling of the wind allowed. He frowned and sucked hard on his cigarette.

I sat back, watching the golden sandstone cliffs of the Sierra de Jaén loom before us and then enfold us in a deep defile, and reflected on how far my friend had come since many years ago we had sheared and travelled together all around Andalucía, working like dogs and living the low life, for a pitiful handful of grubby notes.

When I hung up my shears and dedicated myself to other activities, José stayed in shearing, but learned how to delegate, employing others to do the work while he discovered a surprising flair for organisation. His operation got bigger and bigger, and now he travels every summer to Uruguay to handpick his forty or so expert shearers. He buys their air tickets, deals with their visas and work permits, arranges their insurance, accommodation, everything. Having been a shearer himself; he knows the score, so he treats his men fairly and firmly. He's about the fourth biggest shearing contractor in the country, which does not make him very rich, but means that his boys, as he calls them, shear a hell of a lot of sheep. It's a status that he has to defend fiercely; the world of big contracting is a pretty cut-throat business.

José was still hunched over the phone. He seemed to be getting agitated, really agitated.

'But we did all that stuff,' he said, 'and they accepted it and there was not going to be a problem . . .' And then he exploded. 'It's that *hijo de puta* of a *Búlgaro*. The bastard is trying to fuck us over . . . So what are we going to do about it? What the hell can we do about it?'

He put the phone down and stared at the windscreen, seething in silence. 'What's going down, *primo*?' I asked. 'Who's the Bulgarian?'

The *Búlgaro*, it appeared, was the biggest *pez gordo* (fat fish) in Spanish sheepshearing, and a man you didn't cross lightly. José told me of the dastardly stunt the *Búlgaro* had just pulled, which had something to do with persuading some crony in a high place to insist on a minute inspection of every aspect of Guerrero's Uruguayans' paperwork. José was certain that everything was in order, but it would involve him and his people in a mountain of useless administrative work.

We both watched the road for a while and then José shook out another cigarette and lit it, and reached over to turn the cassette. 'Just you wait, Crease,' he said. 'That *cabrón* is going to wake up one of these days with a red-hot poker stuffed right up his Bulgarian arse and on the other end of it will be none other than José Antonio Guerrero.'

We had been driving for nearly an hour through the ocean of olive trees to the north of Jaén. We zoomed across the muddy Guadalquivir on its long journey down to Sevilla and the sea, and finally left Andalucía through the pass at Despeñaperros, not, as in days gone by, winding down and up amongst the organ-pipe rock formations and the forests, but hurtling across the top of it all on a road supported on towering concrete pillars. It was quicker, of course, and less dangerous, but you couldn't help but feel that something fundamentally important had been lost in Spain's headlong dash to replace every country road with an *autovía*.

And then we were high on the endless plains of La Mancha, stretching all the way to Toledo. We hammered down the slip road into the city, and my hopes of a less headlong rush were dashed as José, still angrily preoccupied with the machinations of the *Búlgaro*, weaved a lunatic course amongst the traffic. We were here, apparently, to visit yet another *pez gordo*, Javier, a man who, as president of one of the biggest sheep cooperatives in the country, held the destiny of a hundred thousand sheep and more in his hand.

'I know this guy a little,' said José, 'but we've got to make a big impression on him today. I've more or less got the job in the bag for my boys, but you never know with that goddam *Búlgaro* trying to poke his nose in. Still,' he said trying to shrug off these dark thoughts, 'Javier's going to buy us lunch and if I know the food in this town it should be a good one.'

We parked where we could, and clumped up the stairs to an office full of files and books, the walls hung with oil paintings of eminent sheep. Nice-looking sheep they were, too – Merinos mostly. Spain's medieval economy was largely based upon Merino wool, and it is still the finest of any sheep on earth.

Behind the desk sat a smooth young man in an impeccable suit. He rose to greet us. This, then, was Javier.

'This is my friend the Eenglish writer,' announced Guerrero unctuously, poking me in the back. 'I told you I was going to bring him to meet you. You've heard of Genesis?'

Javier had heard of Genesis.

'Well, Crease was the drummer of Genesis.'

Javier looked a little bemused, wondering no doubt why I didn't look more like Phil Collins. (Phil Collins had more famously taken my role after I'd been ejected from the group as a schoolboy.) I felt a bit of a berk.

'Did you bring that book from the car, Crease? The one I'm in . . .'

I handed it over. José handed it to Javier. Javier looked at the back cover. 'You must dedicate it to me,' he said, brandishing a biro.

I wrote in the book, something along the lines of 'To my esteemed and admired friend, Javier. I hope you enjoy this book.' Then I handed it back to Javier, who studied the dedication with a nonplussed air. Perhaps it was my writing. Anyway

I figured that that was about all that he would ever read of the book. He thanked me.

'It's not me you should thank, it's Guerrero. It's from him. I just signed it.'

Next there was some business to attend to, and while José and Javier were deep in discussion I tried to immerse myself in the only other piece of literature in the room, the co-operative's yearbook. Now, although I'm as keen as the next farmer on the minutiae of the ovine world, you can only get a certain, limited amount of mileage from a sheep co-op's yearbook. I had, moreover, begun to feel decidedly peckish but reckoned this was no bad thing, as there was bound to be a spectacularly good feed to follow, with all the culinary sophistication one expects from Spain's ancient capital.

At last the tedious business was over and Javier ushered us out and round the corner to a small restaurant. It looked a touch unpromising: in fact, it looked like the typical bog-standard eatery you find on almost any street corner. But the incongruity of this served only to heighten my anticipation. Often (but perhaps, if one is truthful, not that often) you find the most exquisite fare in the most unexpected places. We were shown to a formica table and I winced as the waiter, a large smelly man in a grubby nylon shirt, brushed past me, smacking me in the ear with a stack of dirty plates. The noise from the television, which was perched on a bracket just above Javier's head, was so deafening that I was unable to hear a word of what my companions were saying. More promisingly, though, Javier had begun conferring confidentially with the slob of a waiter.

At length, he turned to me and shouted at the top of his voice: 'Apparently the *hamburguesas* are off. There's only macaroni for starters. The main course is *albóndigas* or *pollo al ajillo*.'

Jeezus, I thought, what sort of a lunch was this to be treated to? Those unspeakable *albóndigas* would be out of a catering tin, chemically salvaged meatballs . . . and the chicken would be slathered in garlic and fifth-rate olive oil. It filled me with nothing but the deepest dread.

Guerrero stared fixedly at the television. The waiter looked expectantly at me for my order.

'Well, I guess it had better be the macaroni and the meatballs,' I said, attempting just the faintest hint of irony.

The waiter shrugged, then hurried off in answer to an imperious ping from the microwave.

I was thinking by now that Javier was less estimable and admirable than I had suggested. I also figured that José was laying me on the line with this pan-Iberian road trip.

I had it out with José as we hurtled a little later through the horrible traffic on the ring road, during one of the cricket's silent spells.

'But of course I'm using you,' he replied with surprising candour. 'It's because you're famous, and you owe it to me, your old mate, to help me out a bit with this, your famousness. After all, you didn't ask for it – and it doesn't cost you anything, does it? – and look what you're getting: the benefit of my company on this trip across the country you've chosen to live in but never get off your arse to see. You can't ask for fairer than that, can you? And me? Well, I need to put my name about and keep it up there in the minds of all my customers. Now generally they'll remember me because I work it that way and I'm a pretty memorable sort of a bloke. But when I've got Mister Famous in tow, and they've got a dedicated book in their office or to give to their mistress, well, they're going to think of nobody but José Antonio Guerrero when it comes to handing out those contracts. You wait and see, Eenglish. It's going to be *pan comido*. So just loosen up.'

To congratulate himself on this subtle mix of sophistry and marketing cunning, he lit another cigarette. I pondered his words a while. Perhaps he was right. Why shouldn't he make some use, if he could, out of my low-key fame? I've been lucky, so why not 'loosen up' and enjoy spreading it about a bit. José's reasonable and matter-of-fact attitude went some way towards restoring my spirits. And so I settled to the task of helping my friend with his winter activity of consolidating gains, muscling in on the *Búlgaro*'s territory, and keeping himself in the shepherds' eyes. I, in my dubious incarnation as Mister Famous, had become the new tool in his kit.

'So where are we off to next?' I asked.

'Just you wait . . . We've got the best part of the day to come yet: we're going to see your fans, Jesús and Eugenia, in Aranda. You're going to love 'em. Oh, and just before we get to Aranda we're paying a visit to Rafael. Rafael is important. He's got a thousand sheep. I sheared them already, but he's a member of a huge cooperative with flocks ten times that size. I really need to get my boys in on it.'

We raced on up the long, long *autovía*, the pale winter sun slipping beneath the hills, the temperature dropping like a stone. Now my purpose had been defined, I was starting to enjoy the journey a little more. An hour north of Madrid we pulled off the motorway and almost immediately into the village of Pardilla.

Rafael's operation was modernity and enlightenment itself. He welcomed us in a great stone-walled restaurant that, beneath mighty beams of oak, served wine from his vineyards alongside milk-fed lamb from his sheep, and the odd suckling pig. It was a temple to carnivorosity that each weekend draws hordes of devotees from Burgos and Madrid. The farm itself was on the edge of one of those tiny villages of Castilla where nothing happens from one year to the next and all the young people head for the cities in search of work and life. Rafael, with his restaurant, kitchen and ornamental gardens, slaughterhouse and distribution operations, employed just about everybody who stayed.

Rafael was about thirty, a driven man, bouncing with enthusiasm. He had just been nominated for an EC award for business innovation. Proudly he showed me the brochure and the papers he was about to submit to the judges. It was written in an unusually lyrical style, aimed at conveying not just the objectives but the very passion of the enterprise. Opposite each page was what purported to be an English translation. 'To visit us', it declared, 'is to wake the bug of livestock and fight with it, to dignify and publicize a career so forgotten, as it is to be livestock.' I could sort of catch his drift, and it was a nice, almost poetic, line of thought. But when he asked, I had to admit: 'It's not quite there yet, Rafael, if you don't mind my saying so.'

He watched anxiously as I read on. The next bit had a slightly sinister, biblical, tone: 'The production is semi-extensive with a pastor who draws the livestock from the beginning, ours is only "flesh".' *Pastor* means 'shepherd' in Spanish and it had clearly slipped through the net of whatever electronic translation service he was using. 'Flesh' seemed to refer to the fact that the lambs were reared purely for the table. There was some succinct culinary advice to follow on the proper utensils and method for preparing his lamb: 'If not used mud pie, we recommend adding a little water. Instructions are for one room.'

'*¿Qué te pasa?*' asked Guerrero, seeing my consternation.

'It's the English. You can't let it go like this, Rafael.'

Rafael seemed crestfallen.

'Don't worry,' beamed Guerrero, 'Crease can sort it all out for you. He's a writer, that's what he does,' and he nodded at me conspiratorially. This would be a tough act for the *Búlgaro* to follow.

'Well, OK. I should be able to do something about it . . .' I agreed, a little hesitantly.

'Good,' said Guerrero. 'My friend here will put it into perfect English for you while we discuss a bit of business.' Like many of my Alpujarran friends, he had no concept of translating or writing being work at all. An hour and a half later, feeling a little befuddled by all the linguistic tangles I'd been unravelling, I joined José and Rafael for some coffee at the bar. 'Come and see the farm,' suggested Rafael.

So we stepped outside, where dark was falling into an icy cold night. The sheep shed was enormous, like an aircraft hangar, but graceful, with soaring arches of laminated wood, a deep bed of clean golden straw, and in the hay-racks the sweetest-smelling hay. There would be worse places, I thought, to be a sheep. As we wandered through these perfumed halls the great door at the end opened and in trooped the flock, eight hundred strong. They ambled in contentedly, their bellies full from the day's grazing out in the fields. José and I sighed as one with deep admiration for such a fine flock of well-kept and beautiful sheep. For all of our differences, this really did it for the both of us. The fractiousness of the day disappeared as we grinned inanely at each other, united in honest admiration of the ewes. Churras they were, with black and white faces, much like a Kerry Hill, but with fine long, almost bouclé, fleeces. We sighed together again.

'They'll be lambing in January,' said Rafael. 'And we wean and slaughter the lambs at around twenty days.'

Twenty days?! That's not even three weeks. I was astounded. We sell our lambs at nine months to a year.

'It's what the market wants,' explained Rafael. 'It's *lechazo* – suckling lamb. If the lamb has ingested anything other than its mother's milk, then it's disqualified; it won't have that delicate flavour and tender texture people want.'

'Well, I suppose that's true, Rafael, but it seems to me such a terrible waste, and even a little barbaric, to slaughter lambs at three weeks old.'

'Depends how you look at it, Crease. They're going to be killed anyway; probably doesn't make that much difference to them when.'

This is a big debate and I wasn't about to go that deep into it right then, so I let it go.

Guerrero nudged me. 'Give him a book,' he said. 'You know, the one with me in it . . .'

Rafael thanked me for the book and looked warily at it.

'I'm afraid I don't have much time for reading – I'm just too busy. I never seem to stop. I'm just going to grab a *bocadillo* now and then I'm off ploughing. I'll probably be out half the night. Thanks very much, though; it's very good of you, but I'm afraid', he admitted with an apologetic sigh, 'I can't see myself reading it.'

It was dark when we crossed the river bridge into Aranda de Duero. We parked the car and walked into the old town, which, even at nine o'clock on a cold November night, was thronged with people. José was looking for a particular bar, where, presumably, we were going to meet Jesús and Eugenia. The cold night air and the prospect of a good meal perked me up and, if I was to be honest, I had begun to look forward to the company of people who were readers. I couldn't help but have a sneaking interest in what they had enjoyed so much about my books and felt it would make a welcome change to shift the discussion from the omnipresent sheep. We traipsed back and forth searching for the right place.

'Ah, this is it,' said José, and we burst from the dark into the bright warmth of a big noisy bar. The Asador de Aranda was a temple to good eating and drinking, with serried ranks of glittering wineglasses, great dark barrels of wine, dishes of indescribable beauty being hurried to and fro, and a hubbub of conviviality and bonhomie; there pervaded a sense of eager and guiltless anticipation of pleasure. This is how it is in the north: they take their food and wine seriously; the waiters and bartenders wear white shirts, waistcoats and bow ties, and are respected professionals.

The torpor that the long hours on the motorway had induced simply sloughed away as I was drawn in by the brightness. 'Ah, there they are,' announced Guerrero, pointing to a couple standing wreathed in expectant smiles by the bar, who I rightly took to be Jesús and Eugenia. They were with a group of friends, and we all kissed and shook hands and bobbed about a bit in the customary quadrille that attends such occasions. A glittering schooner of darkest red wine appeared as if by magic in my hand and the conversation rolled away.

'So, Crease,' began Eugenia. 'Where do you live?' It seemed an odd question. My books are, after all, memoirs about my life in the Alpujarras.

'The Alpujarras, near Granada, like in the books,' I replied, trying not to make it sound too pointed. She accepted the information without comment and, before we could continue, the first *tapa* arrived. It was a potato, a small exquisite potato with a salty crust, and it was followed by more wines and more *tapas*, each more exquisite than the last. Guerrero began holding forth on our day's drive and his latest campaign to put one over on the *Búlgaro*, so it was a little while before I could resume my conversation with my greatest fans.

'Looks like a beautiful town,' I said. 'And the food and wine are terrific. I wish Ana had been able to come and enjoy it, too.'

Eugenia, who oddly enough is not a wine drinker, took a sip of her beer; Jesús finished his wine. They both nodded.

There was a pause, then Jesús asked, 'Who's Ana?'

Eugenia was all eagerness to know, too.

It was my first inkling that Guerrero had been a bit liberal with the truth.

Neither of them, it transpired, had actually got round to reading the book that José had given them. But in the event it mattered not a jot. There was something right about Jesús and Eugenia that I recognised the minute I saw them: an immediate welcoming warmth, which I basked in and returned. And they made wonderful wines. Maybe there is some subtle alchemy that flows through the wine-maker, their vines and wine. I like to think so and, if there is, then it is one more persuasive argument to drink wines from small-scale producers rather than the big operators, in which all trace of alchemy is obfuscated by the industrial chemical process.

So why the gift of wine, then? To cut a long story short, they had read about me in an article in *El Pais*. Guerrero had filled them in and told them that we were friends, and they were thinking of selling their wines down in Andalucía. They were also, quite simply, extremely generous.

* * *

The next day, having stacked the car with crates of wine till it groaned and sank down on its haunches, we began our journey west. I wanted to stay behind and hang out with my new friends Jesús and Eugenia, but Guerrero wouldn't hear of it; he needed me and my famousness to clinch his deals, keep one step ahead of that *cabrón búlgaro*. That was OK: I had loosened up. And besides, there was still a lot of Spain I wanted to see . . . even at 160 kilometres an hour with all the goddamn windows open.

In the next few days we criss-crossed the country, visiting dozens of places, meeting dozens of shepherds and a whole lot of fat fish, leaving them all looking just a little bit baffled and holding a book they would never read.

Our final port of call was Cáceres, way out in Extremadura near the Portuguese border. Cáceres, and nearby Trujillo, are the towns that the *conquistadores*, Cortés, Pizarro and the boys, came from, and enriched with what they pillaged and plundered from the innocent lands and peoples of the Americas. As a consequence they are furnished with a wealth and architectural distinction unusual in towns so small and remote. I had always harboured a desire to visit them, but never made it until now.

There are a lot of sheep, too, in Extremadura, and there was plenty to keep Guerrero occupied in the town. On that day I was not expected to dance attendance in my role of Mister Famous – this was not unconnected to the fact that the fat fish of the Cáceres sheep society was the most dazzlingly gorgeous, auburn-maned woman. Guerrero wanted the field to himself. Accordingly I was despatched to do some sightseeing in the company of Pablo, a sheep farmer who had fallen on hard times and lost his farm.

Poor Pablo was just one more of thousands of victims of the greed and venality of the country's bankers and financiers. He didn't make an issue of it, though, didn't let it get him down, and he was the most delightful guide as we strolled in warm winter sunshine around the beautiful town.

I asked Pablo how he filled his time, now that his farming enterprise had gone down the tubes.

'I keep myself busy with a little of this and a little of that,' he told me. 'I grow a few vegetables, take long walks when I can, and, well, I do a bit of reading,' he added shyly. We were in a bar by now, sipping coffee and grinning in collusion as we observed from across the road the antics of the dastardly Guerrero dancing craven attendance on the beautiful sheep woman. Pablo opened his bag and drew out a well-thumbed and scuffed copy of my first book. 'I was wondering if you could sign this for me,' he added, gazing down at it earnestly.

It had been a beautiful morning.

CHAPTER 14

HOW NOT TO START A TRACTOR

I t's always the same when the Critchley Road Primary School kids come to visit us on their annual trip to Andalucía: the bus driver takes one look at the road and flatly refuses to go any further. The teachers wheedle and implore him for a bit and then they ring me up, and I wheedle and implore for a bit on the phone, but knowing full well that our man is a bit of a jobsworth and is less than keen on the idea of graunching the paintwork on his shiny new bus, nor indeed tipping a score of schoolkids over the side of a cliff. 'They'll have to walk,' he says.

It was a nice day for a walk, but these were city kids and walking wasn't their thing. The remaining journey was about four kilometres, starting with a long steep ascent. They stood on the road and looked up, as if scanning the north face of the Eiger.

'We can't go up there, Miss. It'd kill us,' was the general consensus.

The obvious solution was for me to go and fetch them in the Land Rover, a couple of journeys. It was not much to ask, but I let them stew a bit before setting off, so they could at least make a start on the hill, get a little fresh air, take in the view, before I arrived with the car. On the way I came across none other than Juan Barquero, who was about to load his trailer with firewood. I looked at the trailer and it occurred to me that I could fit the whole lot in on one trip. From a 'health and safety' point of view, this scheme was perhaps a little ropey. But so much, the better.

Juan didn't need his trailer till later in the day, so we connected it up to the Land Rover and off I went, the trailer bouncing to and fro on the rough track and clattering and clanging like the hammers of Hades. A few of the more competitive spirits had actually made it to the top of the hill by Cuatro Vientos, while the rest trailed doggedly a long way behind. As I clanked round the corner into view, a dozen kids fell upon me, panting and wailing.

As I had suspected, they all wanted to go in the trailer. 'I never bin in a trailer before, Mister,' said one lad, as if this was a form of local transport hitherto denied him. Another boy said he would prefer to go in the car with the teachers. 'Very sensible, too,' I commended him, although I thought it was a little unadventurous. Apart from this boy and two of the teachers, Amina and Rukhsana, everybody clambered into the trailer and I shut the tailgate. The level of excitement was palpable, with everybody shrieking and yelling fit to bust and pretending to be terrified. And all this before I'd even started up the engine.

I set off, not so slowly as to be a spoilsport, just enough to give them a bit of a swing and a bounce, but neither so fast as to be unsafe. Of course, it was safe as can be, and Jim the head-teacher was with the kids in the trailer, just in case. Jim told me that he suffered from vertigo, which made his decision to ride shotgun with the kids all the more noble. Now, I have driven this track a thousand times, but it's only when you have a trailer on behind, loaded with raucously screaming kids and a man with vertigo, that you become aware of just how desperate it looks. The track is the most precariously thin ribbon, cut high into an almost vertical hillside, with sheer drops to dizzying depths down in the river below. It's not quite Peru or Bolivia, but it's not far off it. To get them all riled up I put my foot down a little on the straight bits and gave them a bit of a swing around the corners. They loved it and howled and screamed like a bunch of banshees if we came even within metres of the edge. It was a long time since I had heard such a pandemonium of euphoria and excitement. The sun shone; the way was lined with spring flowers; the river was roaring below; the day was getting off to a flying start. Most of these kids had never been out of the city, and the country was putting on a big show for them today.

Meanwhile Ana was at home busily putting the

finishing touches to the lunch. The Critchley Road contingent tends to be heavily weighted with Muslims, which is why in the last couple of years, to avoid a fuss, we have supplied them with Halal chickenburgers for lunch. These went down pretty well, inasmuch as any food is met with enthusiasm by eleven-year-olds. We couldn't face the burgers ourselves, though, knowing, as we do, a little bit about the sort of conditions that those poor cut-price chickens are kept in, the unspeakable stuff they're fed on, and the gruesome manner of their demise. 'You can taste the misery in the meat', in the immortal words of Garrison Keillor's aunt.

This year Ana and I had had a 'discussion' about the burgers. I sort of liked cooking them on the barbecue, and I reckoned that the elemental aspect of the fire and the smoke associated with the food they were eating would be exciting for the children.

'But why should we give them those disgusting things when it goes against everything we stand for?' asked Ana.

'Because it's what kids like,' I suggested.

'Be that as it may, this year we're going to do things differently. I'm going to make them a beautiful floral salad and *tortillas* made with our own glorious eggs.'

'But they'll never eat salad,' I cried, aghast.

'Well, that's what there's going to be; they'll like it once they try it and it'll be a whole new experience for them.'

And so that was that; Ana's decision was final. She also made home-made lemonade with lemons freshly picked from the tree, and biscuits with a face on and chocolate for hair.

Ana had given me instructions to delay the arrival of the kids as long as I could, because the chocolate hair on the biscuit faces was taking longer to dry than she had anticipated, and this had for some reason thrown all the gastronomic arrangements into disarray. The fortuitous business with the trailer, although it had taken the fun factor through the ceiling, was having the opposite of a delaying effect.

I decided to play for time. Halfway along the track, above La Herradura, is a ruined *calera*, a lime kiln. All that remains is a crumbling stone wall half buried among the wild scrub, with the form of a circular beehive. I pulled up beside it and got out. The kids looked at me in open-mouthed amazement.

'This is a culture stop,' I announced. 'Anybody know what this is?' I indicated the ruin.

'It's your 'ouse,' called some wag.

'No, it's a lime-burning kiln. Anybody know what it was for?'

Hardly surprisingly, nobody did.

'Well it was how they made cement in times gone by. They would gather firewood from all around and make a big fire to burn limestone rocks. After a few days of burning, the rocks

245

would crumble and they could be used like cement for building houses and suchlike. These kilns are all over the Spanish countryside and it was probably the lime-burning, as much as the construction of the Spanish Armada, that contributed to the lack of trees. You'll probably have noticed that there are not an awful lot of trees here.'

Nobody had. Why would they? They were from the city; they had probably never given so much as a thought to how many trees there ought to be in the countryside.

To complete the educational element of the tour, I told them the story about the wild boar and how the activities of the *leñeros* had caused their numbers to dwindle until the introduction of butane gas put matters right again.

'Sir, are there boars 'ere, then?' asked one of the girls.

'You're a bore,' interjected the wag, inevitably.

'Yes, lots of them. They're all over the place,' I rabbited on, ignoring the wag. But now everybody was looking around and pretending to see wild boars. These kids had a shorter concentration span than I did. Still, I had won a good ten minutes for Ana and her wet chocolate hair.

I climbed back into the car with the sensible boy and the two teachers, and we set off once more, making a hullabaloo that you could probably hear as far as the coast.

The next delaying tactic was Antonia's *pollino*, the

baby donkey. I parked the car and trailer by the bridge and we set off through the fields beside the river. The grass was deep and lush and shot with buttercups and daisies and poppies. Big yellow butterflies fluttered to and fro amongst the almond trees. By the river was a line of orange and lemon trees, the ground covered with fallen fruit. The kids didn't know where to look first: the river was looking magnificent as it raced and roared down over the rocks. Nobody had ever been so close to a mountain river, and nobody had ever seen an orange or a lemon dangling from a tree before. And then there was the baby donkey.

'Ooh, look! It's sweet . . . Can I stroke it, can I stroke it?'

Stroking Antonia's baby donkey was not really to be recommended, as it kicks and bites. Donkeys tend to be like that. The *pollino* and its mother strolled over to the gate to see about getting some good kicking and biting in. I suggested that we limit ourselves to taking photographs of them, then I managed to divert the kids by saying that they could throw the fallen lemons into the river.

'There's an old gypsy saying,' I told them, 'that if you throw enough lemons into the river, it will turn to gold.' They set to this new task with a will. Throwing lemons into a fast-flowing river is about as good as it gets when you come from Ilford or wherever it is they come from.

'Can I eat a orange, sir?'

'You don't have to call me sir. I'm not a teacher; my name's Chris. And it's *an* orange.'

'Can we eat a orange, Chris? Can we eat a orange?'

'Course you can,' I said, offering this grand largesse with Juan Barquero's oranges. He wouldn't miss a couple of dozen. They were Washingtonia Navels, like our own, the sweetest and juiciest of all the oranges on the planet. Everyone picked an orange. I cut the tops off them and they set to peeling and eating them. Young Darren looked up at me in absolute gobsmacked amazement.

'I've never ever 'ad a orange before in my life,' he said. This puzzled me, but on reflection I supposed that he simply couldn't equate a fruit that grew off a tree with the variety he'd seen in supermarkets.

'Can we swim in the river, Chris?'

'Not here, you can't; it's too fast and the banks are too steep.'

It was mid-March and most of the water was from snow-melt, so it was hellish cold, but I figured that fooling around in the river would occupy another half an hour and – what was more to the point – it would make them happy. So, with some trepidation, we crossed the bridge, and headed downriver towards the ford. Here, apart from the sensible boy and one or two others, everybody took off their shoes and socks, rolled up their trouser legs and leapt into the water, screaming and yelling with delight. I demonstrated how to play 'Ducks and Drakes', skimming flat stones across the surface of the water by spinning them with a deft flick of the finger, in order to get as many bounces as possible. Nobody was half as good as me, which pleased me no end, because normally I am the worst at the game.

Eventually we tore ourselves away from the river and walked up through the farm. By now everybody had become obsessed with the notion of picking oranges and lemons and eating them or sucking the juice from the lemons. Each kid was clutching an armful of colourful fruit. Meanwhile I, with my trusty Opinel knife, was in constant demand for cutting them in half.

''Ere look, 'e's got a knife. 'E's well hard,' I heard one of the kids whisper behind me, seriously impressed.

'It's because he's a farmer; farmers always carry knives,' explained Jim the headteacher, detracting rather from my new-found notoriety.

'Is that your tractor, Chris?' several of the kids asked as we passed beneath the tree that is the tractor's resting place.

'Yes, it is,' I said diffidently. In a certain sense I suppose the world may be divided into those who possess tractors and those who don't. The vast majority, of course, fall into the latter category.

'Really, your very own? Is it a real one? Can we 'ave a go on it? Please Chris, please . . .'

'Not now. It's time for lunch.' I figured the

chocolate hair would be dry by now. The year before, the tractor, a rather appealing red 1960s model Massey Ferguson 135, had been the star of the show, eclipsing even the river and the oranges. The kids had fooled around with it all afternoon.

We passed through the gate to the pool. The water was the deepest dark brown from the tannin in the million or so fig leaves that had fallen in the autumn. Ripples and wavelets marked the disappearance of the myriad creatures who lived in its depths – frogs, toads, turtles, snakes, water-boatmen, pondskaters and so on. They could all see what kind of crap was about to go down and had decided to make themselves scarce. Very wise, I thought.

I told the children about the toads, and added, perhaps unwisely – but I wanted these kids to have a memorable experience of everything – that the skin secretion from certain toads can work as a hallucinogenic and that some people lick them for this reason. This was a piece of half-baked infor-mation that had somehow come my way. I was banking on the idea that being city kids it was pretty unlikely that any of them would catch a toad, let alone lick it.

I was wrong. Just as I said this, a number of toads, up for an adventure, made their way up to the surface and started hanging out on the top step . . . and a certain Maya, who I had thought one of the more timid kids, grabbed one of them and held it up for everybody's inspection. Given the poor press that toads get, and the fact that they are not the most endearing-looking of creatures, I thought she did pretty well. She gripped it gently but firmly as if she had been a toad-handler all her life. All the other kids gathered eagerly round her.

'Go on, lick it!' shouted Darren. 'Yeah, lick it! Lick it!' came a chorus behind her, loudest as always from the back. 'No, you lick it,' replied Maya quick as a flash, shoving it towards Darren's face. Darren, who was having a big day, what with his first ever orange, took it and gave it a thorough licking. Funnily enough, the toad did not seem to mind at all.

'Sir, I'm 'allucinatin',' he cried, wheeling around and making odd looping movements, while erratically rolling his eyes. Jim shot me a look, anxious and stern. 'Pack it in, Darren. You're fine. And put that toad back, Maya . . . and you too, Mustafa,' he added. 'This is not the way we treat animals in class six.' The man had eyes at the back of his head.

Soon Ana appeared, coming along the garden path accompanied by the dogs. The delaying tactics had worked well and she was wondering what on earth had happened to us.

'This is Ana,' I said. 'My best friend.' As I had expected, this occasioned some confusion, as the idea of your partner being your best friend is far from universal.

'I thought she was your wife,' somebody said. 'Wot, aren't you married, then?'

'She is and we are, but we live so far from the known world, and there's just the two of us, so she has to be my friend, as well.'

This seemed to satisfy them.

'Ugh, wot's that?!' shrieked one of the kids pointing at Bumble and backing fearfully away.

Ana introduced the dogs, who were turning themselves inside out with the most ingratiating tail-wagging. Their craven and wormlike demeanour had the effect of immediately disarming the nervousness that a few of the kids felt about dogs. Bao and Bumble always do well out of occasions like this, as they get an awful lot of attention and, even better, they get fed at the table by the kids, something that we never do. Had the dogs been involved in the menu negotiations, they would probably have gone for the halal chickenburgers, though, rather than the omelette and salad.

Slowly, in a long line, we all wended our way up the steps to the house. Another surprise: this was not the sort of house that our new friends were familiar with.

'Is this really your 'ouse, Chris?' asked one.

'It certainly is,' I replied.

'It's really small,' one girl observed.

'Actually it's a bungalow, innit?' suggested another. 'My gran's got one just like this.' Which surprised me. I hadn't imagined that northeast London went in for vernacular Alpujarran architecture, topped with grass rooves.

'Well, I suppose you're right; it hasn't got an

upstairs. And yes, I guess it is rather small, but then there's only the two of us, and we don't take up that much space. And most of the time we live out here on the porch; the house is just a place to go and get things from.'

A kilo or so of crisps vanished in fifteen seconds flat, and then there was Ana's exquisite home-made lemonade in a multicoloured selection of plastic mugs. There were cries of delight. It wasn't fizzy, but it was fresh and lemony with mint and cinnamon and really like no other lemonade. It, too, disappeared in a matter of minutes.

At this point Ana laid out two enormous and beautiful omelettes – deep, deep yellow from the home-laid eggs and bursting with peas, onions, potatoes and mint. They were works of art. And to top them off was a huge salad bowl with the richest selection of salad leaves and herbs all gathered fresh that very morning from the garden, and garnished with the most dazzling array of petals – purple malva, blue borage, and bright yellow and orange marigolds. It looked so beautiful, it almost broke your heart. Amina, Rukhsana, Jim and I gasped in utter delight.

'Eugghh! I'm not eatin' that. You can't eat flowers. Yuck,' said one of the boys, as I had expected.

There was a mutter of general agreement. 'Yeah, flowers are poisonous; everybody knows that,' added another well-informed soul.

Somehow we managed to persuade the kids of the harmlessness, and even the desirability, of eating

these particular flowers, and, helping ourselves to
tortilla and salad, we adults went to sit at a distance
with our beer and wine, leaving the kids to thrash
it out for themselves. In the event the food made
quite an impression on them, but they didn't eat
an awful lot of it, mainly because they were already
so stuffed with oranges and lemons. Also they were
pretty excited and wanted to get off and fool around
on the farm. Jim, Rukhsana and Amina tucked in
happily – it was a fine moment of respite after all
their labours, first in finding the necessary funding
and permissions for the trip, and then shepherding
their gang of pupils to Spain.

'Please, Chris, can we 'ave a go on the tractor?'
   'Please, Chris.'
   'Sure, take it for a run,' I said. The teachers
gasped in horror, as one.
   'It's OK,' I reassured them. 'They'll never start it.'
   'I bet we can,' said Jessica. 'I bet we can start it.
What about a hundred pounds if we do?'
   This was a cool kid. I looked her in the eye and
said: 'Make it a thousand.'
   The teachers and Ana looked at me in conster-
nation. Actually, if there was one moment at which
the day started to take a slightly darker atmos-
phere, it was the moment of that injudicious bet.
Of course, I was on firm ground: there was not a
snowball's chance in hell of their starting the
tractor, even though the key was in the ignition.
With the Massey Ferguson 135 you have to have

254

the transfer lever in the neutral position to get the starter motor to turn over; the stop button must be in, and I always leave it out when I turn the tractor off. If they did manage to fathom out those two anomalies, then there was probably not enough go in the battery to start it up. There wasn't much fuel in the tank, either. But, even so, if there were by some chance enough battery and enough fuel to get the engine running, they would have to raise the heavy cultivator on the back, then switch over the hydraulics to raise the front end loader. Then, and only then, would they be able to move the tractor. My money was safe.

But Jessica galloped off shouting that I had offered them a thousand pounds if they could get the tractor going. They could share the money between all of them.

We adults were on to our coffee by now, and we sat in the warm sunshine and talked, while a strange quietness settled on the farm below. The whole gang of them were gathered round the tractor, pooling their combined knowledge of mechanics to try and get it going and thus clean up on the thousand quid.

They started to appear in twos and threes, confabulating earnestly in whispered tones.

'We've got it going,' someone said . . . but I knew they hadn't, for I was listening with all ears and I hadn't heard a thing. Then Jessica appeared on her own and in tears.

'They say they're not going to give me any of

the money because I didn't have anything to do with getting the tractor going,' she snivelled.

'Yes, but you brokered the deal. You'll be the one who distributes the money . . . in the unlikely event that it comes to it,' I assured her. Thus comforted, she dashed back down the steps to where the action was.

Somebody else came up.

'It 'asn't got any oil in it,' he said. 'We've 'ad to put some oil in it, an' then we got it going.'

I suppose this should have sounded a warning bell, but I assured him that they had not got it going as, if they had, I would have heard it.

'We did; we did.'

'No, you didn't.'

Only then did I start to realise that I was up against some pretty shifty kids, who would stop at nothing to get that money off me. I wriggled a little uncomfortably in my chair.

There was the sound of some excitement from down below, and a few minutes later a delegation arrived, muddy and ruffled and slightly malodorous, with the news that Mustafa had broken off the ignition key.

'Well, bang goes your thousand pounds, then,' I said. This wasn't quite as bad as it sounded, as another one of the anomalies of the Massey Ferguson 135 is that you can switch on the ignition with the dipstick.

'No, but we got it going before he broke the key. We put some oil in the tank and started it up. It didn't have any, but we found a barrel marked "oil" and we put that in the tank and then it started.'

Being absolutely certain there were no barrels of oil in the vicinity and that none of the barrels anywhere on the farm were marked 'oil' anyway, I simply smiled at this. Clearly the kids were so steeped in subterfuge, they no longer knew where the truth lay.

'That's quite enough horseplay for now,' intervened Amina, surveying the wretched state of their clothes and grimacing a little at the mucky farm odour they seemed to give off as a group. 'It's time to wash your hands and get ready to head back.'

Luckily there was the trailer ride back to the pick-up point to distract the kids from their disappointment of 'being robbed', as they saw it, of a cool thousand quid. And with all the rumpus of the first ride, subdued just a tiny notch through tiredness, we carted them off the farm.

On the way back I went down to have a look at the tractor and inspect the broken key. There was an odd, yet familiar, smell coming from the vehicle that I found hard to place but which started me wondering, as I should have done earlier, about this 'oil' they had got hold of. I wondered some more for a while, and then I saw it. Next to the tractor was a white plastic drum that the kids had somehow dragged up from the garden. This was quite a feat, as it was actually a forty-litre drum, although by no means full. It was empty now.

For my Valentine's Day present four years ago, Ana had given me, along with a little pot of pansies, a zinc bucket. The bucket was to pee in, and the idea was that I would pee in the bucket every day and in the evening pour it into a drum. Here the priceless urine would ferment and eventually become a fantastic nitrogen-rich (and impressively malodorous) compost activator. By this means I would be returning to the soil something of what we took out of it. It was a really wholesome sort of ecological scheme, and the beautiful simple ecological logic of it thrilled me. It had taken a long time to fill the forty-litre drum. Then I had hidden it in a shady part of the garden to ferment before I poured it on the compost heap. It had reduced by half over the years and was by now an unspeakably vile, brown, thick, smelly liquid.

With some trepidation I unscrewed the cap on the fuel tank and sniffed at the contents. The Massey Ferguson 135 is powered by that miracle of British engineering, the Perkins three-cylinder diesel, an engine that will run for ever under whatever conditions of maltreatment you care to subject it to. I was dead sure the children would have been unable to start the engine before, but now I was absolutely certain; even the doughty Perkins would be hard put to start with a tank full of well-fermented piss.

CHAPTER 15

SANTA ANA

Not so long ago the idea of a book group in Andalucía would have seemed about as likely as an orchid in a peat bog. But times have changed and it seems that a whole generation who would not have thought of picking up a book are now avid readers and eager to meet authors at readings and literary festivals. And it's not a pursuit limited to the young, either, for whom Harry Potter opened the magic door. All ages are at it, and there are book groups everywhere, from the fabled cities to the humblest of *pueblos*.

When my books were first published in Spain, the invitations came in thick and fast – and, of course, at the start I went along to them all, delighted at this acceptance of my writing in my adopted home. But as any author will tell you, book events demand a whole lot of time, for not very much return. You do them for love and duty, or because something catches your eye. And so it was with the invitation from the reading group of Domingo Pérez, a village hidden amongst the cornfields to the north of Granada. Their letter reached me at one of those times when I was casting around – as I do from time to time – for an excuse to down tools and take the day off. I looked idly at the map and realised that Domingo Pérez was near Fuente Vaqueros, the birthplace of Federico García Lorca, the great poet and dramatist murdered by Franco's henchmen in the civil war. I could make a pilgrimage of it, turn it into something of a literary trip.

So, in the fierce heat of August, with a hot wind pouring through the open windows, I pulled out of Santa Fe and drove between fields of tobacco, maize and asparagus towards Fuente Vaqueros. The rutted road was laced by channels of the most unappetising and evil-smelling grey water in which a few frogs croaked. Very occasionally another car passed by, but it was getting on for lunchtime and nobody with any sense was out under that bleached white sky. There were some tobacco-drying sheds gathered in a huddle round the edge of the town, then some houses, not that different from the tobacco sheds, and finally the town itself.

My talk to the book group was not due to start till six, and Domingo Pérez was only an hour's drive away. The afternoon hours stretched out ahead of me. How best, then, to honour the great poet?

I parked beneath the shade of a plane tree in the square, put my hat on and climbed out of the car. A couple of bars were doing no business; there was nobody about. There were hamburgers and pizzas on offer but it was just too darn hot to eat, and a pizza seemed a poor way to mark a visit to Lorca's town. I set off walking down the road, heading to nowhere in particular, ducking in and out of the shade of the plane trees. On and on I walked, beyond the main street and past a scattering of deserted tobacco sheds. Tobacco, it seemed, was the thing in Fuente Vaqueros. The sun beat harshly down on my hat and shoulders; a fly kept station with me and settled from time to time on my nose. I screwed up my eyes against the glare and trudged doggedly on. As I neared the poplar grove outside town, I turned along a track, intending to make a square of my walk back into town, but the track petered out in a farmyard and I had to go all the way back and retrace my steps. With the best will in the world, this was hardly the sort of walk to conjure up poetry.

Coming back into town, I finally came upon Lorca's house. It was closed, predictably enough, and nearby was a bar with a woman stacking chairs and taking them inside. She told me that times were hard and there was not much custom. I could have told her that. She said she would serve me a drink, but I didn't really fancy sitting there on my own while the chairs were stacked up around me. I thanked her and returned to the car.

Fuente Vaqueros was as dead as towns get in the Spanish summer – and I knew its neighbours would be no different. But there is something about these one-horse towns, deserted in the afternoon sun, that is oddly appealing, and I set off for the nearby

261

Dehesas Viejas, with the idea of lunching there. I had been there many years ago with Domingo to buy barley straw and had not imagined that I might return. Domingo told me later that his sheep wouldn't touch the stuff. He reckoned the straw had been stored downwind of a dung-heap and been tainted with the smell. We'd been had, he said, although my sheep tucked into the straw enthusiastically – or, at least, as enthusiastically as one might tuck into a meal of barley straw.

In the bar in the plaza, a short man and his son, who had an arm in plaster, sat on stools and half-heartedly watched a huge television at top volume.

'Do you want a *menu del día*?' shouted the youth behind the bar.

'Just a *ración* of something, nothing too substantial.'

'We've got *carne en salsa*,' he said.

So I had meat in sauce, and a *clara*, a shandy, and went to sit beneath an awning in the deserted plaza in order to avoid the moronic drama on the telly. As I sat down, in an excess of consideration, the youth behind the bar switched the sound through to the external speakers, in case I felt lonely eating out there all on my own with nothing to listen to.

It was the hottest hour of the day and the meat was salty and the bread like cardboard, but the *clara* was cool and sweet. I took a notebook out and thought about what I might say to the book group, but it was difficult to think straight. A dog slunk down the street; a cock crowed; a fly settled on the remains of my meat in sauce; the sun burnt through the thin awning. Sleep came stealing down upon me.

I managed to fight it off; I had some way to drive and then I would need to summon up the energy for my talk. So I left Dehesas Viejas and drove east along a minor road that wound through the corn-fields. The harvest was almost ready, the oats and barley in ear and casting that wispy sheen across the folds of the hills. In the distance on all sides were mountains, barely visible in the heat haze. The sun, still almost vertically overhead, blazed down, so that the wind that blew through the windows was laden with the scent of herbs and hot corn. Occasionally the blank whiteness of the fields was relieved by silvery green olive groves, but there was no sign as far as the eye could see of towns or villages.

I ought to come upon Domingo Pérez soon, I thought, and then suddenly there it was, hidden in a hollow, a little red-roofed town gathered along a dry river flanked by ilexes. I cruised slowly through the empty streets. It was five in the after-noon and I still had an hour to spare, so I headed up the river in search of a spot for a siesta. There was a blanket in the back of the car, and a cushion, kept there for just such eventualities and, after a few unpromising starts amongst the thistles and the burrs and thorns, I established a base in the shade beneath some willows. I lay down on my back and slipped straight into a deep hot sleep.

When I came to, I experienced one of those glorious

moments of nothingness and unknowing, when for an infinitesimal span of time you are utterly liberated from your earthly identity and have no idea who or where you are. Above me there were willows, and the whispering of a warm breeze in their leaves. I squinted up at them, wondering what I was supposed to be doing here, and all too soon remembered . . . and, oh lawd, it was nearly six o'clock and time for the talk to the readers of Domingo Pérez. I hauled myself to my feet, brushed the burrs and thorns from my shirt and trousers, splashed my face with a bottle of spring water, hot from the car, and headed off to do my turn.

I reflected a little on the literary life as I wound slowly among the ruts and potholes of the country road. Here I was, a writer driving through a summer afternoon in Andalucía to give a talk to a reading group. The notion seemed bizarre; I had lived for most of my life from manual work and I still find it hard to think of writing as 'proper work'. And yet, books have played a huge part in my life. At school I rarely read more than was required, but because Margie, the love of my teenage years, lived in rural Dorset, I developed a passion for Thomas Hardy. Together, Margie and I would moon around the beautiful Wessex countryside with blanket and books, steeped in glorious adolescent lust and doomed bucolic romance. It might not be too far-fetched to think that Hardy steered me towards becoming a shepherd; modelling myself, in the way that one does when one is young, on Gabriel Oak in *Far from the Madding Crowd*. And, perhaps because I was so steeped in rural romances, I did not read any political stuff until much later. So when my contemporaries were manning the barricades in Paris in 1968, I was lolling in the long grass with Margie on the chalky downs of Cranborne Chase. I couldn't help it; I didn't know . . . and you have to read the books to know.

And then came the book that cast the die for me: Laurie Lee's *As I Walked Out One Midsummer Morning*, his irresistibly romantic account of walking through Spain in the summer of 1935, in fierce heat and on the eve of war. From then on my path was set. I would become a bohemian, write poetry, go wandering in strange lands – and most specifically Spain. I wasn't the only one. Laurie Lee had that effect on probably hundreds of young people back in the 1960s and 1970s.

I owed my fascination with Spain to two other books, too: Gertrude and Muirhead Bone's *Old Spain* and Gerald Brenan's *South from Granada*. The latter, at least in part, directed me to the Alpujarras. Brenan settled in 1919 in the village of Yegen – then several days' mule ride from Granada – accompanied by a library of two thousand books. There he read and wrote feverishly, and entertained the likes of Virginia Woolf and Lytton Strachey from far off Bloomsbury.

Old Spain I came upon by chance in Guildford, when I was labouring on a nearby farm. The town had an antiquarian bookseller called Traylens – one of those bookshops that was not obviously open to the public, with a bell you had to ring to seek entrance. As I passed by, my eye was drawn to a huge leather-bound book, propped open to show a pen-and-ink drawing of a courtyard in the Alhambra. I rang the bell and, after a respectable lapse of time, the owner opened the door and peered at me without enthusiasm. I told him I wished to look at the book in the window.

The book, which I leafed through while the antiquarian hovered by my elbow, was the travel diary of two artists wandering through Spain in the 1920s. The drawings were exquisite, both in subject and execution. So this was Spain, the land south of the Pyrenees. I had to go there and see it for myself. I turned over a few more pages, and then made a decision. 'I'll have it,' I said.

'I'm afraid this a very rare limited edition and rather expensive,' the bookseller whispered gravely. 'I cannot offer it for less than one hundred and twenty pounds.' It was a staggering amount, but I was smitten. I asked if I might put down a deposit of five pounds and pay the rest in instalments over the ensuing months.

And that's what I did. I saved all the money I could over the next six months and then returned to Traylens to claim my book. I have it to this day, and the spell it cast upon me sent me south after the harvest was in, hitch-hiking first to Dover, then Paris, then working the *vendange* down in Cognac to help pay for the journey, and finally slipping across the border at Roncesvalles and making my way down onto the plains of Navarra. That was more than forty years ago. The power of books: they have made me think what I think, live where I live, and be who I am.

Ana, too, I reflected. In fact, it may have been her declaiming poetry by the fireside in a pub in the wintry Surrey countryside on our first date that made me think she might be the right sort of girl for me.

Then, before we left for Spain, we both agonised over how we were going to support our thirst for reading in the out-of-the-way corner we'd found. This of course was long before the days of online book-buying. Our lucky break came just a few days before we set out, when we came upon the Crawley Lions' Club fundraiser. They had stuffed a church hall with books and, wandering in, Ana and I were like kids in a sweetshop, pouncing on new titles and old favourites, tottering to and fro with stacks wedged under our chins, until at the end of the morning we had amassed a couple of hundred books. The whole lot cost us less than twenty pounds and we loaded them into our trailer, throwing out extraneous pots and pans and lamp stands to make room.

At El Valero we cleared out the room on the roof, known as the *cámara* – the only dry outhouse we had, where the previous incumbents had stored their salt, maize, hams, cereals and beans – and set to work putting up shelves and arranging our haul in some sort of order. Then we stepped back and considered our library, wondering if we would ever find time to read them.

All of this, I thought, might provide some material for the talk.

I entered the town, found the venue and parked the car. As I had suspected, it was not exactly Carnegie Hall: it was, in fact, a primary school. A couple of jolly women, shortish and rotund, were going in as I turned up.

'Are you the writer, come to talk to us?' they asked, in that wonderfully unselfconscious way that the Spanish have.

'That's the way it looks,' I said diffidently. We introduced ourselves. They said they were *encantadas* to meet me but I sensed somehow that they were just the slightest bit disappointed. Perhaps I wasn't quite up to the author photo on the book, or lacking in writerly gravitas. It was hard to pin it down.

We moved into the classroom where the event was to take place and my heart sank. It was like an echo chamber, each sound horribly magnified and distorted by the nature and texture of the walls, floors and ceiling, and taking long agonising minutes to dissipate. I found it impossible to make out what anyone was saying, or even what I was saying myself. Chloé's classrooms in Orgiva were like this, too, and I had often thought it a wonder that she or anybody else had ever been able to hear anything, let alone learn. Ana and I had been along to a couple of those evenings where the teachers talk to you about how wonderful – or not – your child is, but, given that we had been unable to make out a single word that was said to us, we abandoned the practice and never went again, thereafter ignominiously accepting Chloé's own reports of her aptitude as a pupil.

The noise in this classroom was right off the scale, as a couple of dozen women and a bevy of young children were giving it all they had got. But as I tried to work out what was going on, a good looking middle aged woman in a track suit grabbed me by the hand and, pulling me down towards her, kissed me on both cheeks. So far so good, I thought. Then she looked around in apparent consternation. 'But where's Ana?' she asked. 'We'd hoped you'd bring Ana along to meet us.'

'Ah, I'm afraid she couldn't join me. Ana's home at the farm, looking after the animals.' It was an excuse of course. Authors don't normally turn up to readings with the cast of their books in tow, even if they are married to them.

'*Ay que pena*. She's at home looking after everything,' sighed the tracksuited woman, shaking her head before retreating to share the disappointing news. It wasn't quite the boost you look for at a public appearance but I've learnt to expect this sort of response from women readers. In fact, we have come to call it the 'Santa Ana effect'.

Ana is by a long head the favourite character among my Spanish women readers, who empathise with her attempts to inject a little reality into my blithely optimistic plans. I can't cavil at this, as Ana is a favourite character of mine too – it's why I took up with her. One of the great privileges of writing is that people lend you their imaginations and enter emotionally into the world you describe. But it's a rum thing when they assume that, despite my having introduced them to everything they know about Ana, they have a better understanding and appreciation of her qualities than I do. If Ana comes across to them as more patient, wise, steady and well-judging than me, then surely that's because I have told them so.

By now everybody was moving chairs and desks around, and the crashing and trumpeting as the chair legs graunched on the tiled floor, and everybody yelled suggestions as to the best way to arrange the seating, sent the noise level clean through the roof. I was placed on the teacher's platform and sat there like a lemon, attempting to collect my thoughts, when I became aware of a woman mouthing something at me, the content of which was entirely lost in the appalling din. She seemed to be gesturing at a mobile phone she was grasping in her hand. I grinned at her and gave her a thumbs-up, in admiration of her phone, though it looked to me a fairly standard model and not worth holding up a literary talk over. At this she shook it with renewed urgency, as if she wanted me to take it from her. I looked at her quizzically. What, in the name of the Host, could she be after? I put my hands in my pockets. I didn't want the damn telephone. I had seen enough of it. But still she looked at me beseechingly, shaking it ever more insistently.

I reached gingerly out to take the phone, as if it were a snake in a box. I don't like my own mobile phone, let alone other people's and I looked at it suspiciously. The evening sun was streaming through the windows and I couldn't see a thing, just a black screen with motes of dust.

The phone owner, who seemed to exercise what passed for authority here, called imperiously for silence. 'It's Celia,' she shouted, and, as if the words exerted a mesmerising influence, the room fell suddenly still . . . you could hear a pin drop, or at least a football cannoning off the door at the back where the kids had retreated.

'Ah, Celia!' they all cried gladly.

It was like this: Celia was the woman on the far end of the telephone. It was she, as founder of the book group, who had set this gig up, but at the last minute she had had to go into hospital to redo a botched operation on her leg, poor woman. So I was to speak to Celia using this device in front of my audience.

Now, this is not the way I like to do things. When using the phone I prefer to seek the privacy of a quiet corner or, for preference, a telephone box. But there was no way out of it: I could hardly refuse, given that the poor woman was in hospital and, if the owner of the phone was to be believed, she was dead keen to speak to me. Accordingly I raised the accursed object to my ear.

'*Hola*, Celia,' I said hesitantly. Two dozen eaves-droppers craned forward expectantly.

I thought I heard a distant croak . . . but perhaps not. I tried again. '*Hola*, Celia. *¿Qué tal?*' How's it going?

Not too good, I would have imagined, given that she was back where they had already botched up one operation on her leg. But what do you say?

This time there was a distant croak, as of a person a long way away in a hospital ward talking on a mobile telephone. Of course, I was quite unable to make out what she was saying. I adjusted the phone to get my ear nearer the actual hole where the voice ought to come out. The audience was getting excited now, egging me on to new feats of telephony. I smiled ingratiatingly at them, then thought better of it and put on a hospital sort of a face, full of mournfulness and concern. I listened for a bit to the indistinct croaking of the device. After a while I decided to say something. 'Well, it certainly is good to be here in Domingo Pérez,' I hazarded. 'It's a shame you can't be here with us, though, Celia. How's the leg?'

A certain amount of sighing from the audience gave me the impression that things weren't perhaps too well with poor Celia's leg. And then all of a sudden I got the hole in the right place and I could hear Celia clear as day.

'I'm so pleased you have been able to come,' she

was saying. 'Is Ana with you? I'd love to hear her voice.'

'Er, no, I'm sorry. Ana's at home.'

'Oh, what a shame, our readers will be disappointed; they really were looking forward to meeting her.'

More mournful looks from the audience confirmed that this was, indeed, the case. The phone, as phones inevitably do, had started to break up, allowing me an entirely acceptable, if rather clichéd, excuse for bringing matters to a close. My attempts to do so were more or less drowned out by all the women in the audience shouting greetings and encouragement to poor Celia and her leg. The noise had returned to its former deafening levels. I returned the phone to its owner, who had been leaning into my ear beside me.

It was time for the talk. I spoke for a bit about how I had come to write a book and what it all meant to me, and then read out a couple of short passages. I had made it clear at the beginning – as if this were necessary – that I preferred a conversation with everybody joining in, as opposed to a monologue with myself, so, except for the time when I was reading, it was pretty hard to get a word in at all.

My adrenalin, or whatever it is that enables one to make a fool of oneself in public, carried me through this ostensibly solo part of the evening, and when the time came to announce questions, and throw the baton entirely to the floor,

I sighed and stretched with relief, ready to relax as the 'questions' rolled.

The beauty of talking to Spanish readers is that they generally prefer the sound of their own voices to yours, and most of them have come along to get their own oar in rather than just to sit passively. They can't help it; it's the way they are. So, when you open the talk to questions, a forest of hands rises from the audience. And the questions tend to take the form of long and convoluted statements, endlessly qualified and elaborated upon. 'My question', the false questioner might begin, 'has three parts', or five, or worse. Of course, by the time the so-called 'question' grinds to its end, a period that can last as long as twenty minutes, you have entirely forgotten what the beginning was about. But that doesn't matter, as nobody really wants an answer anyway.

This evening, however, proved slightly different.

A hand shot up ahead of the others. It belonged to a thin woman with thick spectacles sitting at the back. She had not joined in the general hubbub hitherto, but now she looked me in the eye, cleared her throat and, without any preamble, asked an unusually concise and carefully considered question: 'How does your wife put up with you, that poor, poor woman?'

'Ay yes, she must be a saint,' concurred three or four more voices.

'Santa Ana,' someone said . . . as I knew they would.

CHAPTER 16

ORANGES AND LEMONS

One autumn afternoon a certain Manuel Martín Archilla turned up at our house; he was a man of unexceptional stature and was accompanied by his six-foot-four son. He had, he told me, been born at El Valero fifty-seven years ago, and lived the first six years of his life here. 'There was an almond tree there,' he said, as we exchanged opening pleasantries, 'and this is where my father kept his goats . . . but everything is much smaller than I remember.'

I showed him around the farm with some pride, but also a touch of embarrassment as I indicated each trapping of luxury and lasciviousness – running water, telephone, gas cooker, a hammock strung between two trees . . . broadband Internet aerial. He followed me around slowly, sometimes shaking his head in what I supposed was wonderment.

'There were five families living here back then,' he announced. I thought this over for a moment, and calculated that it would probably have meant twenty-five people living where now there were just the two of us, with occasional visits from Chloé, rattling about like peas on a drum.

Not only that, but those ten parents and fifteen children would have lived almost entirely off what the farm could produce. The 1940s and 1950s were years of wretched deprivation in the countryside. There would have been no cash to buy anything beyond the basics; there was barely enough for clothes. Domingo's mother, Expira, had told me that at six years old she was sent out barefoot on the hills, amongst the thorns and flints, tending the family's goats. And because she had no shoes she could not go to school, for the Church, who ran the dismal excuse for an education system, stipulated that you had to wear shoes to go to school.

'This is where my family lived,' exclaimed Manuel, 'and in there lived my aunt and her family. There used to be another door here, and another family lived in there.'

The room in which Manuel's family had lived was our larder, a tiny outhouse which we had reclaimed from rats. It has no windows, just a small skylight, and the room is half-cave, built into the rock. In one corner is an old wine-press; in another a bread oven. It was hard to imagine how a family could have fitted in here.

Manuel did not make any judgements. He didn't go on about how lush and lovely we had made the place, nor did he excoriate us for sullying the primitive but pristine world he had known with our modernities and urban aberrations. I thought that he would like to potter about a bit on his own, so I disappeared into the kitchen to do some chores, telling him to make himself at home. He thanked me with a smile as he wandered away, followed doggedly by his bemused and rather beautiful son. The poor boy had only ever known the urban whirl of Barcelona, and was making heavy weather of feigning interest in where there had been an almond tree or a big pomegranate – or where goats or chickens had had their being fifty years ago.

A little later on, Manuel came back to take his leave. I wanted to talk to him for a bit, ask him a whole lot of questions about how life had been back in the 1950s, but he could not stay, he said, as his wife, who had absolutely refused to cross the bridge and had no interest whatever in country life, was waiting for him in the car.

'I do remember the oranges, though,' he said. 'El Valero always grew the sweetest of oranges, and I see that you are looking after the old trees.' This was true. We have been putting a lot of work into the trees, grafting better varieties onto the indifferent ones, pruning drastically, working well-rotted dung and compost into the earth around their roots, and being assiduous about regular watering.

Just before Manuel left, I remembered to ask him, 'Can you cast any light on the origin of the name, El Valero?'

He looked at me in surprise. 'Yes, of course. The farm was named after my grandfather, Paco Valero, who lived here.'

'Just that?'

'Just that.'

It was a rather disappointing conclusion to the mystery. However, I thought to myself, the farm has always been known for the quality of its oranges. I'd always suspected that: our Washingtonia navels are about as delicious as a delicious orange gets.

When we first arrived at El Valero, we wanted to work the place properly as a farm. It was both our dream and a necessity; we had sunk what money we had into buying the place. We were younger then and bursting with energy, and we threw ourselves vigorously into the work.

Under the censorious supervision of Pedro, the previous incumbent of the farm, whom we had somehow acquired along with the land, we harvested each and every orange and lemon we could get hold of. This seemed the right thing to do, as everybody in the village of Tíjola down the road was harvesting their citrus. It took us four days. We stuffed the beautiful fruit into huge hessian sacks and hauled them across the river to where the buyer from Lecrin Valley Citrus was waiting with his lorry and his *romana* – a primitive 'hook, weight and bar' scale in use since Roman times to weigh the harvest. We got 11,000 pesetas for the entire crop; roughly fifty quid.

It was a far from encouraging result: fifty quid wasn't very much even in the 1980s, and it felt like scant recompense for the eight man-days we had spent on the job. But undeterred we set about trying our hand at the summer almond harvest. The almond trees on the hillside above the farm had been more or less abandoned and so many had reverted to bitter almonds, as they do in the wild. Actually, it was a bit more troublesome than that, as they often had some branches of bitter almonds and some sweet. Now, you can't tell the difference between a sweet almond and a bitter one just by looking at it; you have to taste them. And, worse than that, it takes time for the bitterness to develop in your mouth, so you have to make a proper job of mastication, really grind them up with those molars. Then and only then do you know if you've got a sweet almond, which is as subtly delicious as a nut can be . . . or a bitter almond, a thing which all of a sudden fills your mouth with the vilest bile, tasting intensely of cyanide and vomit. Forgive me, but that's the way it is with a bitter almond. They are good for nothing – or almost nothing. Curiously enough, a tiny proportion of bitter almonds is added to the sweet to give flavour to marzipan.

You can get used to anything, though, and it was said that the old folks of the Alpujarra developed a taste for bitter almonds, to the extent that there were, for many years, posters published by the state against the practice. Twenty bitter almonds will kill you, they said. For they don't just taste of cyanide; the *amygdalin* in almonds is converted by enzymes in your stomach to cyanide itself.

Naturally it fell to me to check out the almonds, to sample each tree for sweetness or bitterness. Ana would watch me for telltale signs as I masticated furiously. If my features were suffused with sweet relief, we would spread the net and attack the tree with our long canes; if, as was more often the case, I started to gag and retch and spit out the bitter, bitter paste, we would move on, pick another representative-looking almond, and I would squat down and crack it open with a stone and bite into it.

Of course, I don't know what cyanide tastes like, but bitter almonds certainly taste like what you imagine cyanide would taste like. And by the end of the first morning I had such a god-awful belly-ache that we decided to abandon the almond harvest altogether. In years to come we would lop the almond trunks just above sheep height and graft onto them good sweet varieties like Marcona, but that year I wasn't going to go down with cyanide poisoning just for the handful of pesetas that our miserable crop would bring in.

It seemed unlikely that we would be able to make anything but the most meagre living from the fruits of the farm, so for years we muddled along living off our wits, the income from sheep-shearing, seed-collecting, and whatever else happened to come along before we happened on a lucky crop of books. As for the oranges and lemons, well, we helped ourselves to what we wanted, and just left the rest on the trees for the beauty of it.

Somebody once asked me – in the way that people do – what I most loved about living in Spain. I pondered for a bit, considering the culture, the people, the sunshine, the architecture, the music, the cities, the landscape (there are a whole lot of good reasons to enjoy living in Spain). But eventually I came to the conclusion that the one thing I really could not do without was having my own orange trees. Apart from the beauty of those gorgeous oranges shining from amongst the deep, dark foliage, there's the delight of idly picking one as you pass a tree, and meditatively peeling and eating it segment by segment. Things have reached such a pretty pass that I can't bring myself to eat an orange even if it's been in a bowl for just one night – it tastes stale. It's the same with orange juice – we have to squeeze our own into the glass.

Citrus trees are unique and extraordinary in that they bear ripe fruit for many months of the year, at the same time even as the blossom and the tiny ripening fruit of the next crop. We eat the first of our oranges at the end of November, and we are still picking them from the tree and eating them at the end of June, when they remain firm and juicy, although there tends to be quite a high incidence of maggots in the fruit by July.

As for lemons, well, they fruit nearly all year round, although by the end of August they are well past their best. This manifests itself in a most curious way: the pips start to germinate and, when you cut a lemon open, you find tiny green lemon trees inside, complete with roots and leaves. It seems beyond belief that anything can live in, and be nourished by, the sharp acidity of a lemon. At this stage they also start to taste rather disagreeable. Juan Barquero has some late lemons by the river, though, and these tide us over until our own trees come back into production. Lemons, of course, are another thing I would not want to be without.

When the wind blows in the winter, which it often does, it knocks the ripe oranges off the trees. With a strong wind they fall in thousands, and the earth beneath the trees becomes a carpet of fallen fruit – orange, obviously, and lemon-yellow beneath the lemon trees. It's disheartening to see a large part of your winter's crop lying on the ground, but the sheep are in heaven. I let them out of their shed in the morning and they gallop off as one, an amorphous woolly mob racing round the terraces hoovering up the fallen fruit. The funny side of this is that sheep have only a lower set of teeth, so that when they bite into the oranges, they get them stuck on their teeth – and they can be dislodged only with difficulty. Sometimes the whole flock can be seen standing around in a state of bafflement and confusion, each sheep with an orange stuck firmly on the end of its nose. We, who live so far away from our fellow man, are easily amused.

A darker side of this becomes apparent the next day, though, when you find the flock lurking in the sheep-shed, too lame to walk, their flanks heaving, and looking miserable. Fortunately this phenomenon doesn't last long, and a few hours later all trace of lameness will have vanished. It is due to the citric acid, which goes straight to their joints. I believe musicians are urged to avoid orange juice for this very reason, in case they can't hold their instruments.

I suppose it's possible that the sheep weigh up the pros and cons and decide that it's worth putting up with the temporary lameness for the exquisite delight of the oranges; there are not so many exquisite delights in the life of a sheep. On the other hand, maybe they just forget, and each time they see that carpet of fallen fruit they think it's the first time. I have read that fish can remember things for thirty seconds (what, one wonders?), and sheep, love them though I do, are not that much higher up the evolutionary scale than fish.

If you're lucky enough to own a farm, albeit a not entirely feasible peasant farm that you maintain mainly for the pleasure of the sheep, you can't help feeling that it ought to be able to produce crops for people beyond its incumbents, and at least defray its running costs. Ana and I believe fervently in this dream and we have kept El Valero ticking over, hoping that one fine day we might no longer just live on the land, but from it, too.

After long and careful consideration, Ana decided that there were two ways in which we would achieve this goal. We would apply for organic certification, thereby increasing the market value of our produce, and we would greatly develop the fruit-growing potential of our land. Oranges were the obvious crop to start with, as we knew these were of a high quality, but once we'd established our market we'd expand into pomegranates, a fashionable miracle food that had the advantage of growing spectacularly well in El Valero soil.

In Spain, to become organically certified, you need to have kept your farm free from agrochemicals and petroleum-based fertilisers for five years, to ensure that no residues still linger in the soil. From the beginning of that period no product must be used that is deemed unacceptable by the governing body, the CAAE (Comité Andaluz de Agricultura Ecológica). This includes seeds – which must be from organic sources – as well as fertilisers, pesticides and sprays. You also have to keep a book in which to note down assiduously all your agricultural operations and activities. Once a year an inspector comes to snoop around the place for signs of any of the forbidden chemicals and check that you have filled in the requisite pages.

Given that we had been running the farm on sound natural and ecological principles for the last twenty years and had not only banished agrochemicals but had been derided by our neighbours for doing so, we should have been rather smug about these checks. Yet, unaccountably the thought of the inspector calling left us apprehensive. There's something about being inspected that triggers a guilty consience, even if the visit involves nothing more than a morning entertaining an idealistic young man, brimming with interesting ideas gleaned from agricultural college.

The usual pattern is that we wander round the terraces counting trees and sheep; pick some fruit and eat it; then have coffee together while he tut-tuts over the fact that we haven't filled in the operations book . . . and then we fill it in together, with careful fabrications. It's hard to remember exactly when you did what, and, indeed, why. Finally he signs us off and walks back to his car with vows of undying friendship and a bag of earth for analysis, to make sure there has been no skulduggery.

The sheep, though they tick almost all the organic boxes, are kept out of the equation as I'm loath to fully commit to a regime that might leave them defenceless against their fiercest or most tenacious foes. Take fleas, for instance. There will always be fleas about if you live amongst cats and dogs and sheep, and most of the time they are manageable, but every so often – and there's no knowing when – some mysterious combination of elements causes them to multiply exponentially, and what you get is a nightmarish explosion of the flea population. It starts in the sheep-shed, where one day you walk in and look down to find your legs and trousers literally black with fleas. You rush out, tug off your trousers and submerge them in a bucket of water with a big stone to keep them down. Meanwhile, the dogs go in for a nose round in the sheep-shed, and come out caked from head to toe in a living mat of fleas. The dogs sleep in our bedroom, and within days the connubial bed itself has become what the locals call a *pulgatorio*, where a *pulga* is a flea. You can't sleep at night for the tickling of hosts of tiny creatures all over your body, and your every waking hour becomes a torment of itching and scratching.

And even the water treatment with the trousers is to little avail. I have left trousers beneath the water for ten days, only to discover when I put them on again that they were still alive with fleas. The cunning creatures creep into the tucks and seams, where there may remain the tiniest air pocket, and there they hole up waiting for the day. When you put the trousers on, they lie low for a bit, until the warmth of your body awakens whatever notions it is that fleas have, and they come skittering out of their hiding places and head for the warmer and more enticing parts of your body, notably your nether abdomen. And there they play havoc with your parts, doing whatever foul things it is that they do.

You can't mess about with fleas. It's no good spraying them with preparations of mares' tail, nettles or garlic soaked in spring water; you've got to hit the bastards hard with some virulent chemical.

Similarly it's no use pussyfooting with the intestinal parasites to which sheep are prone; you need strong stuff to combat these. The sheep graze, when not on the hill, in a river valley: ideal conditions for parasitical snails, which they ingest with the plants that grow in the riverbed. In order to keep the flock in good health, we have to zap them at least once a year.

Fortunately, the sheep don't seem to mind being left out of the organic regime. And it matters not a jot when it comes to selling them, as we have more than enough customers with a taste for hill-and herb-reared lamb.

You might imagine that after a wait of five years there would be some sort of fanfare about making the grade as organic fruit producers – a ceremony, perhaps a little like getting a university degree, with capes and mortarboards, to welcome you into the exalted community. Yet all we received from CAAE to confirm that the conversion process was complete were a stack of new forms to fill in, more pages in which to note down our agricultural activities, and some stickers. These sport the CAAE logo – a green leaf and a yellow celestial orb. It didn't seem much, and yet in the days that followed I noticed a subtle shift in my estimation of our farm and, by association, my self-esteem as a fruit grower. Our oranges had undergone no greater change than ripening slightly from one day to next, yet they seemed to glow with added lustre. All of a sudden they were no longer run-of-the-mill oranges from a mountain farm, but properly certified organic fruit – more prized than, say, the identical crop hanging from identical branches on Juan Barquero's side of the river.

If truth be told, though, I'm a little unsure about organic farming: I believe that without the agro-chemicals the land takes less of hammering and that with careful and thoughtful management the soil should become ever more productive, ever richer with humus, and easier to till. I also believe that the soil is, along with the fish of the sea and the forests, one of the fundamental inheritances of man, so looking after it properly is unquestionably the right thing to do. But I am unconvinced that it can feed the population of the world. It's hard to imagine how the great grain-growing prairies of Russia and the Americas can be farmed without the addition of artificial fertilisers, nor how the quantities of food necessary to feed the burgeoning urban billions can be produced with the addition of nothing more than compost and dung.

However, a tiny mountain farm like ours does not lend itself to the practice of agribusiness, and so, gladly, and perhaps appropriately, we have gone organic. And indeed, a few weeks after the stickers arrived we got a call from Federico, our local representative of an ecological fruit-buying company based on the Almerian coast. At least, that was what we *thought* he said. It was hard to know exactly, as he insisted on speaking in a bizarre approximation of English, with random German- or Dutch-sounding words. It seemed that the only language he was unwilling to hazard was his own. After several false starts, he eventually used just enough Spanish for us to infer that he and a man called Antonio, possibly his boss, would come the following Tuesday and take a look at our fruit.

A couple of days later, Federico and Antonio came clattering over the bridge. Antonio, a short, solid-looking man, dressed in blue overalls, had the quiet authoritative manner of an experienced farmer. He seemed hugely relieved to discover that we spoke Spanish and immediately fell into a discussion with Ana about her plans to develop fruit growing on the farm. Meanwhile Federico bobbed and weaved around us, interjecting the odd comment in cod-English.

Antonio was a man who liked to keep his cards close to his chest, but even he seemed impressed by our Washingtonias. Everyone is. 'How many kilos can you give me of good, unblemished fruit?' he asked, gazing thoughtfully up at a tree through the thicket of leaves. We estimated about five hundred and, after a few more questions, impeded by a few more unfathomable sallies from Federico, we finally struck a deal. He would pay us a euro per kilo.

This sounded to us like good money, certainly

more than we'd ever been offered in the past. Antonio had also shown an interest in the pomegranate harvest – an up-and-coming market, apparently – although being a citrus man himself he offered to put us in touch with a pomegranate expert when we felt that the trees were ready. The fruit market is highly specialised in this way.

We harvested the oranges and lemons on two warm sunny days in March. Antonio brought us a couple of hundred plastic crates, and Ana, I and Christophe, a French friend and enthusiast for organic farming, set to the harvest. We started with the lemons, picking only the perfect ones. If you see lemons on sale in shops and markets, you may be unaware of the extremely varied morphology of the lemon. There are some really weird lemons about, in particular what are known as 'Hand of Buddha' lemons, which resemble nothing so much as an octopus. Occasionally you get one of these aberrations on a normal lemon tree. Others are less spectacular, but still too weird to be considered acceptable. Lemon trees have wicked thorns, too, and many fruit are damaged by the effect of the wind rubbing the fruit on the thorns. So all in all only about sixty percent were acceptable to the buyer. The rest we left on the trees.

Christophe and I climbed ladders and clambered about in the thorny trees, filling sacks tied around our waists with what we thought were the most perfect fruit. Then Ana, down on the ground, would inspect each one and put it in a crate for selling or in a reject sack. As one might expect, her word was final, and nearly every time we tried to argue the case for a marginal lemon, our plea was rejected.

We filled about thirty crates with perfect, gleaming, yellow lemons, and then started on the oranges. It was the same process, except that we have many more orange trees and they are, if anything, even more thorny. Ana again subjected the picked fruit to the same draconian selection process, and at the end of the second day we loaded the crates onto the back of the Land Rover and drove them across the river to where Antonio was waiting. He was impressed by the rigorous quality control Ana had instigated. It looked like the harvest would bring in a profit at last – not huge, but a sign that the farm might begin to pay for its upkeep.

As well as our harvest, we ended up with dozens of sacks filled to the top with slightly blemished oranges. This would have been depressing if we hadn't already done a bit of research and discovered that the food bank in Granada was only too pleased to take any oranges that were spare – and they didn't give a tinker's toss about the blemishes. These city food banks are feeding millions in Spain at the moment and they need every bit of help they can get. It felt good to know that none of our labour would be wasted and that the reject fruit would have its own social value rather than having to be discarded like the windfalls.

In celebratory mood after delivering the properly shaped citrus to Antonio, we packed the Land Rover again, this time with the sacks of misshapen but equally delicious fruit, and drove off to Granada. The food bank was in a shed-like building in the centre of town and staffed by a small gang of volunteers, most of them recent immigrants from Africa or Latin America. As I parked up alongside, two tall Nigerian men and a sturdy-looking Colombian woman hurried out to help unload the sacks. They had made a large holding pen for the produce out of stacked tins and milk cartons in the centre of the hall, and tipped the oranges in to form an appealing centrepiece. 'These'll be gone within a couple of days,' they cheerfully told me.

Rounding the bend to the river track on the way home we noticed Domingo hard at work in the field beside his house. Domingo, despite initial scepticism about organic farming, had also begun the conversion process for certification and had only another two years to go. Since gaining the deeds for the farm he had been working tirelessly, fencing in and cultivating parts of his land for his latest projects: the expansion of a nursery special-ising in local Alpujarran plants and the cultivation of a small plantation of goji berris, a shrub of Chinese origin, for the wholefood market.

Like pomegranates, goji berries – which are sold dried, the fresh berries having a curiously bitter aftertaste – are considered a superfood, supposedly packed with all manner of antioxidants and healthful qualities. I tend to creep past Domingo when he's hard at work on the plantation for fear of being invited to come and sample the crop. The berries really do taste much better dried and even Domingo's enthusiasm for them has diminished slightly after reading on the Internet that they need to be harvested wearing rubber gloves, as contact with human skin taints the fresh fruit and turns them black. Nobody likes wearing rubber gloves, especially when it's hot (and in the Alpujarras it's hot most of the time), and it's not quite the done thing for us farmers to be seen wearing such prissy protection.

El Valero, as I've made clear, is blessed with some of the finest oranges you can eat – the Washingtonias – as well as an inferior type, the sweet orange *dulces*, which are best left for squeezing. In addition, we have a few bitter orange trees dotted about. These were either there when we arrived or, in some cases, are sweet orange trees that have reverted. Bitter oranges, or Seville oranges as they're known in Britain, are the wild form of the orange, and their rootstocks are used to take grafts of the less hardy, more delicate, eating oranges.

The thorns on a bitter orange tree are fierce, and the flesh and juice of the fruit is more sour than the sourest lemon. This, along with their hardiness, is why it is the bitter oranges that are the tree of choice for urban planting. Bitter orange trees gladden the streets and squares of Spanish cities with their beauty and their scent, and of course, because they are more or less inedible, urban man feels no need to nick the fruit.

I say they are more or less inedible, but they are wonderful for cooking. The juice is sharper and bitterer than a lemon, and the zest, as well as tasting of orange, has that delicious quality of making your mouth tingle and water at the same time. This accounts for why they are the perfect fruit for making marmalade. And bitter orange marmalade, it occurs to me, is of fundamental importance to human existence; I breakfast upon it almost every day of my life.

Bitter orange juice also makes a fine substitute for lime or lemon when it comes to *ceviche*, which happens to be my favourite way to eat fish. There's also an exquisite Middle Eastern dish of minced lamb cooked in bitter orange juice, and then there's bitter orange ice cream; and, finally, a lemon drizzle cake made with oranges.

There are those (my own mother is one) who would have it that a drizzle cake is not a proper cake at all, because it doesn't rise like a sponge. But, for my part, I don't give a stuff for sponge and I defy anyone to come up with a better use for bitter oranges. My 'bitter orange drizzle cake' lurks like a toad in the bottom of the tin, thick and dense and heavy and wet with bitter juices – you really cannot imagine how delicious it is. Here's the recipe:

Ingredients
Zest and juice of 3 bitter oranges (or lemons
if you are unfortunate enough not to have
any bitter orange trees to hand)
2 eggs
175g butter
225g dark brown sugar
125g raisins
25g desiccated coconut
150g wholemeal flour, preferably with nuts
and grains and stuff

Method
Melt the butter and mix with 175g of sugar.
Add the orange zest, raisins and coconut.
Stir in the beaten eggs. Fold in the flour.
Bake in hottish oven for 35 minutes.
Make the drizzle by warming up the juice
and stirring in the other 50g of sugar.
Puncture the cake all over with a chopstick
(thin end) and drizzle (hence the name)
this sugary juice into the cake.

Eat while warm.

CHAPTER 17

ALL THE FUN OF THE FERIA

The thing about being an expatriate is that you come to believe that you alone have true insight into your adopted land, its customs and idiosyncrasies. You are convinced that your command of the language is better than that of other expats, and you tend to wince and look away whenever you encounter one of them making a bad fist of speaking it. You also fondly imagine that your friends amongst the natives are more interesting, more authentic and just plain better than everybody else's. Now, of course, this is moronic nonsense that arises from an expat's insecurities – but it's the way it is. And the flipside is an almost craven gratitude for the slightest mark of approbation from your Spanish neighbours.

A few years ago I was lamenting to Carlos the municipal policeman that, if I lived here for the rest of my life, I would never be like a native: I look like a *guiri*, I lamented; I talk like a *guiri*; I even behave like a *guiri*. (*Guiri* is a slightly pejorative term for a foreigner.) 'No, no, no Cristóbal. Look at me,' he said, presenting me with a fine view of his dark aquiline features. 'Why, I'm a *forastero*,

297

too' (*forastero* means somebody from outside and in his case his forebears were from Morocco). 'We're all *guiris* here: we've come from all over and, besides, you're one of us now; you have sowed your seed here.'

Carlos was referring, with a nice touch of bombast that is typical of the Spaniard, to the birth of my daughter, Chloé. From an expatriate's point of view this made me feel pretty good. Imagine, then, my delight when Mari-Ángeles, mayoress of Órgiva, asked if I would deliver the *pregón* – the opening address – for the town's annual *feria*. The *feria* is the high point of the year in the town's festive calendar. For four or five days, everyone gives themselves up entirely to the urban pleasures of drinking, queuing for the giant communal paella and dancing *pasodobles*.

It occurred to me that Mari-Ángeles was perhaps scraping the barrel a little with her choice of *pregonero*. Perhaps there was nobody else who would do it, despite the rewards of a free bar tab – which is a pretty good emolument as it doesn't take you and your friends long to notch up a fairly spectacular bill. And obviously, nobody wanted a repetition of the previous year when the town's official chronicler delivered a *pregón* that went on for no less than two and a half hours without pause. The Spanish – and this is one of my pieces of privileged expatriate insight – are much given to pomposity and prolixity. But even in Spain two and a half hours is two and a half hours and, at the opening of a *feria*, it's two and a quarter hours hours too long.

So there it was. I had been chosen to deliver the *pregón* and, after feeling rather puffed up and pleased, I fell into considerable anguish. Normally, as you may have gathered, I go for spontaneity in public speaking, relying on the arrival of the muse in the nick of time to get me out of whatever hole I have dug for myself. Sometimes she'll be there, whispering sweet inspiration; sometimes she'll leave you in the lurch. Muses are like that. But it works more often than otherwise.

This time there was a bit more hanging on the event. So I took the sensible precaution of asking Augustín at the bank what a *pregón* should consist of. He considered for a minute, before declaring: 'The most important thing is that it should be brief and lighthearted, a joke or two, to get them on your side. Then you have to thank everybody for anything you can think of, all the most excellent dignitaries who will be crammed up on the stage behind you, and flatter them a bit, and then finally hit the audience with a theme.

'A good *pregón* ought to be a bit like foreplay,' he added. 'Something to get everyone in the mood and build up a bit of anticipation before the main event.'

I noted all this down assiduously.

The day eventually arrived and found me surprisingly relaxed. This was because I felt I'd nailed the theme part. I had hit on *convivencia* – the coming together and living in relative harmony of the different cultures that create the rich and noble mix of modern Órgiva society. And I had actually written and memorised a speech, with which Chloé, who is good on accurate Spanish idiom and takes it upon herself to edit out anything that she considers embarrassing, had lent an editorial hand via email and phone.

Chloé herself would be arriving on the day from Granada with a posse of friends, although she wasn't sure if she'd be there for the start of my speech, as she had an earlier assignment, oddly enough, as a pallbearer. It was part of a protest against the cuts in education, which involved her and her friends whitening their faces and processing through the city streets with a cardboard coffin in which lay the mangled cadaver of Spanish public education.

The Órgiva *feria* takes place at the end of September, so, against the unlikely event of rain, they erect a huge marquee in the Plaza de la Alpujarra, with a stage up one end, a bar down the other and, in the middle, a great rabble of plastic chairs and tables around a dance floor. I was due on at seven, when the *feria* officially started, although in truth the festivities had already been swinging for some time, with the parading around town of the three beauty queens – adolescent, senior and infantile – accompanied by the oddly named 'Mister Órgiva'.

At seven in the evening darkness was beginning to fall, so the lights were all on and the generators thundering away, and the gilded youth of Órgiva were galloping around the town in gangs, and the old folks were already getting tanked up in the bars, each of which had shelled out for a monster-decibel speaker-stack which blared out a selection of music seemingly selected by stone-deaf socio-paths. The noise level was like a fairground. Of course, it *was* a fairground.

I was hovering about for my *pregón* duties well before time and at about eight fifteen was ushered on stage. Apart from football, everything always kicks off late in Spain – and with a *pregón* that's perhaps no bad thing, as by now the townsfolk were well oiled and I too had made modest inroads on my free bar tab – a little whisky for the voice, followed by a couple of red wine chasers.

The ceremonials went like this. First the town dignitaries filed up onto the stage: Mari-Ángeles the mayoress, followed by the various councillors – culture in a slinky black dress; urbanisation, finances and environment each smartly besuited; sports in a clean tracksuit. These people would hover behind me, yawning, rocking back and forth, and grinning at their friends while I delivered my peroration. You would have thought that they could have had something to sit on, but no, they had to stand, which was doubtless why they were keen to avoid a repetition of the historian's *pregón*. I lurked on the edge of the stage, grinning inanely while Mari-Ángeles warmed up the crowd and introduced me.

Was I nervous? A bit, I suppose. 'No man is a hero to his valet,' said Winston Churchill. I've given talks all over the place but home territory is a tough act, with the Spaniards not entirely convinced that you are speaking Spanish, and all the other expats turning out in the hope of seeing your downfall. And in Órgiva there are heaps of expats, most of them vocal critics and masters of scepticism, who are convinced (with a certain amount of justification, in this case) that, whatever it was you did, they could have done it much better themselves.

There was a half-hearted ripple of applause from the floor as Mari-Ángeles came to the end of her introduction and offered herself for the customary mayoral kiss. I kissed her warmly – and perhaps a little too moistly – on both cheeks. I moved to the microphone and tested it with a euphonious bit of throat clearing. I normally like to go for the deep abdominal voice production and do without the microphone – I have a loud voice – but here, with the cacophony of *feria* clattering all around me, it had to be the microphone. I stood as tall as I could, tucked my belly in and, beaming ingratiatingly at the public, began.

'*Hola, Hueveros!*' I shouted. 'Hallo, Egg-People.'

I should explain. The Spaniards enjoy an inordinate fondness for the place where they were born, not so much to the country itself so much as their province, and above all else their town or, indeed, village. Thus, around our neck of the woods, you see car stickers that say '*Yo* ♥ *Granada que es mi tierra*' – 'I love Granada, which is my land'. It's hard to imagine people having stickers with 'I love Basingstoke, which is my land'. We the English don't have that same attachment, which may be why we have always been such travellers and explorers. The Spanish, convinced of the superiority of their land over all others, have tended to stay at home, except, of course, for the people of Trujillo and Cáceres in Extremadura, who would take off from time to time to distant continents in search of gold and silver to replenish the coffers of family, Church and State.

All Spaniards return home to their village for the annual *feria*, no matter if they live at the far end of the country; they're like eels to the Sargasso in this. And as a consequence they have names for the inhabitants of every city, town and village in the country. Where we have Londoners, Mancunians and Yorkshiremen, they show more imagination, often giving a nod to distant history: thus the people of Cádiz are *Gaditanos* and those from Huelva are *Onubenses*, Gades and Onubes being the names of their respective towns under Roman rule. Elsewhere the derivations can be more obscure, as in the people of Órgiva being known as *Hueveros*, Egg People.

Apparently, back in the mists of time, a king of Spain took it into his head to pay a visit, somewhat unaccountably, to Órgiva. The townsfolk were so poor that they had no bunting to hang in the streets so some bright spark suggested that they hang garlands of broken eggshells to lend a festive air. This they did and it pleased the king so much that the people of Órgiva were known as *Hueveros* ever after. An alternative and pleasingly conflicting explanation is that some time in the 1920s the unpopular Alfonso XIII passed through the village and the people threw eggs at him.

And so, following my greeting, I started my *pregón* with this story. Most of the townsfolk, I was told later, had never heard it . . . and in fact I can't remember where I got it from, so it might not have cut the mustard with my predecessor, the *chronista*. Still, it was short and sweet and seemed to go down quite well – or as well as any story can go down above the loudspeakers and alcohol-fuelled hollering that passes for conversation at *ferias*. But, as often happens after a good anecdote, I found myself losing the thread. I couldn't quite remember how I was supposed to get from here to the main part of the speech. Luckily I had my notes, so I shook open my glasses, hooked one end over an ear (a sad pass to come to) and peered down at the scruffy and much-folded page before me. There was one word underlined helpfully at the top. 'Foreplay,' it said.

Foreplay . . . What the hell was that about? I couldn't for the life of me fathom it out. I stared at the word for a bit, conscious of the yawning of the dignitaries from behind . . . and then the penny dropped.

Perhaps it was the whisky which had by now hit its mark, or perhaps it was just the relief of remembering why I had written it but I found myself announcing to the good citizens of Órgiva that a *pregón* ought to be like a sort of foreplay before the *feria*, something to get the anticipation going. From a shuffling amongst the audience, a pricking up of ears, a graunching of plastic chairs on concrete, I inferred that there was some interest in what I was saying.

'The sexual metaphor,' I rabbited on, 'is appropriate, because when you get to a certain age, you may find that the imagining and the anticipation of sex is actually better than the act itself, for to be truthful there are not so many occasions on which it is ever going to be as perfect, as agreeable to both parties, as uncomplicated or as pleasingly hygienic, as one had planned. And there lies the problem of the *pregón*. If I do my job properly and whip you all into a frenzy of anticipation, then we run the risk that the *feria* itself will be a terrible disappointment.'

There was at this point the nearest thing to a stunned silence that you can get in a municipal tent, as my audience struggled to understand why I was doing down the *feria* . . . or, worse, confiding to all and sundry that I was a bit of a letdown in the connubial department. I caught an anxious look from Ana and Chloé, who had made it from the funeral of education. But I was in too deep by this point to do anything other than wade on.

'I had a friend', I continued, 'who would go to concerts and listen to the orchestra tuning up. He loved that anarchic, random sound, as all the strings and tubes and skins that constituted the instruments of the orchestra slid up or down from wherever they had been to meet finally in one great glorious harmony. Then, as soon as the musicians had finished tuning, he would get up and leave. "Nothing", he said, "that the orchestra could do afterwards, could possibly compare with the sweet anticipation of the tuning up."'

Even I could see that I was heading for the rapids here. I cast down again at my scrap of paper for rescue. 'Thank the dignitaries,' it said.

Now, I am told by my daughter, who is a person suspended between the worlds of Englishness and Spanishness, but more critical of the English, that we English have the vice of saying 'thank you' much too often. But it has to be said that, when it comes to formal speeches, the Spanish are in a different league: they name everyone by name and thank them till they're blue. I looked behind me at the gently rocking row of dozing dignitaries. I'm not good at names, particularly in Spain, where a certain paucity in the name department means that almost everybody has names that are confusingly similar. Mari-Ángeles I knew . . . but was it Mari-Ángeles Vílchez Martín or Martín Vílchez? As for the other dozen or so dignitaries,

I knew that there were liberally spread amongst them Garcías, Vílchezs, Ruizs, Morales, Romeros, de la Torres, Almodóvars and de Almodóvar Sels . . . preceded by a seemingly random selection of Antonios, Isabels, Marías del Mar, Josés, Pepes, Pacos, Vanessas and Manolos. But I couldn't for the life of me remember in which order they went, nor to whom they referred.

I hedged. I would do something new, taking advantage of the prerogative of being a *guiri*. After all, what are *guiris* for but to effect changes in the stagnant status quo? Turning towards the municipal worthies, with a sweep of my arm I offered a great all-encompassing blanket of thanks.

'If you feel you deserve a little bit of this great body of gratitude, please feel free to take it,' I announced to the company assembled behind me. 'It's big and it's cheap, and there's plenty of it.'

And so finally I turned to my theme of *convivencia*. This has become something of a buzzword in Spain and is used by social commentators to look back on that state of harmony and tolerance that supposedly extended to the three communities – Muslims, Jews and Christians – back in the days of the Caliphate of Córdoba. *Convivencia*, of course, came to an end pretty sharpish after the conquest of Spain by the Christians. But one lives in hope – and perhaps Órgiva is a beacon. For some unaccountable reason, we have just about the richest mixes of nationalities in the peninsula. There are Algerians, Argentines, Americans,

Chinese, French, Germans, Romanians, Czechs, Moroccans, Sahrawis, Poles, Dutch, Lebanese, Uzbeks, Iranians, English, Swedes, Danes, Bulgarians and Turks . . . to say nothing of the more local *Zamoranos*, *Leoneses*, *Madrileños*, *Jiennenses*, *Gaditanos* and *Onubenses*.

I told my audience that when I arrived here, twenty-odd years ago, the mix was not quite so rich. There were a few Danes and Dutch, and some English scattered thinly here and there. The *Alpujarreños* were generally quite interested to observe these foreigners with their strange habits, although there were one or two who did not see it as a good idea. My neighbour Domingo once went to town to buy some *habas* to sow. Our Dutch neighbour, Bernardo, asked him to buy a bag for him, too. Arriving at the seed merchants, Domingo said: 'Give me a kilo of *habas* and another for Bernardo.' The manager looked at him and said: 'I don't sell to foreigners.' 'OK,' said Domingo. 'Make that two kilos for me, then.' Such simple little acts are the roots of *convivencia*.

'Things have changed,' I continued, warming to my theme, 'and I believe they might have changed just that little bit faster and in a more imaginative direction as a result of the richness and variety of the mix of ethnicities and nationalities. I wouldn't say that all change comes about as a result of *forasteros*, for perhaps the very best of those who seek to change and improve the life of the Alpujarras come from local families, but I do believe that the mix of races and nationalities provides a strong impulse for change and improvement.

'There are still, of course, those who refuse to accept the benefits and mutter in the gloomier corners of bars about the foreigners who come and muck things up for the others . . . but there always have been types like this. No doubt,' I suggested, 'there were some grumpy old Ibero-Celts who would have said the same of the Phoenicians. The less progressive Phoenicians would have moaned about the arrival of the Greeks; the Greeks certainly would have complained about the Romans, and the Romans been equally sniffy when the Visigoths moved in. When things started to go wrong for the Visigoths, and the Berbers turned up to sort things out, there were those who saw it as a bad thing. For seven hundred years things went more or less alright, until the *Reyes Católicos*, the Catholic kings, came along and the denizens of Granada would mutter to themselves how things had been going along perfectly well until these latest foreigners arrived and mucked things up again.

'And each of these successive invasions,' I insisted, 'brought with them their own innovations to enrich and enliven the land they had settled. The orange tree, for instance, and the olive, the aubergine and the almond, tobacco; Christianity, Islam and Christianity again; the dome, the horseshoe arch, the patio garden, the lovely Alpujarran village.

'And I'm proud to be a part of this village,' I continued. 'A village that understands more than most about *convivencia*, because, although there are difficulties and things are not always easy, you, admired *Hueveros*, have more than a full measure of tolerance and patience. And you know, in the best traditions of this blessed country, how to enjoy and benefit from the influence of new arrivals.'

I glanced once more at Ana, who was holding up a glass of whisky and grinning at me. A sure sign that I needed to bring my *pregón* to a close.

'So, at the risk of talking and behaving even more like a *guiri*, thank you, *Hueveros*, for making us welcome in this patch of paradise for the last twenty years; thank you, *Hueveros*, for looking after and playing with my daughter in the alleys and patios of the village, and making of her childhood, and our lives, a time of joy and pleasure. And thank you, too, *estimados Hueveros*, for the inspiration you have given me over the years.

'*¡Basta ya de pregón!* Enough of the *pregón*. *Hay placeres que nos esperan.* There are pleasures awaiting us. *¡Al timón!* To the tiller!'